Overcoming Difficult Situations and Survive

Sandra Niche

Published by Niche Creation Publishing in 2022

Second Edition

ISBN: 978-1-7397011-09

www.nichecreation.co.uk

Niche Creation Publishing

Dedication

To all women and men in society who have been affected by domestic violence and have survived. Also, for those sisters and brothers who are struggling to overcome. I am pleased to dedicate this book to you to encourage, strengthen, empower, motivate, and help you rise to another level. The level that will not only change your lives but the world you live in.

Whilst journeying throughout different stages of my manuscript, I had to come to terms with certain types of struggles faced by women within a male-dominated society. Physical, psychological, emotional and mental abuse may well have destroyed me, had it not been for the Grace of God.

In my quest to broaden the spectrum attributed to domestic violence, I am not refraining from identifying the male counterpart since they too, have been on the receiving end as documentary evidence suggests. Let us hope that certain sisters will be inclined to take stock of repercussions arising from physical, emotional and psychological abuse levelled against some of our men.

Domestic violence affects every culture, class and people of all status. Remember, you are never too young or old, rich, or poor to experience an assault on your own dignity and rights to individual freedom.

May this book bring to all who read through its pages, hope and renewed inspiration in the face of one woman's courage to overcome the forces of domestic violence, school bullying and other related issues of abuse.

ACKNOWLEDGEMENT

I would like to give special thanks to God, the Creator who has conferred upon me the strength and ability to write this book. Commendations also to my two younger children who have been my rock throughout this journey. Not to forget my two older daughters who are part of this journey, because they were born into this equation.

PREFACE

This is the first copy of *Overcoming* and I pray this will inspire and bring revelation and deep conviction to those who are blind to the type of moral questions tied-up with day-to-day situations we often take for granted.

I am convinced that the true-life factors emerging from the pages of my book, will give insight into ways forward in one's quest to embrace change, especially where they are confused.

Finally, it is an honour and a joy for me to recommend this book to you the reader. Moreover, I trust that in the wake of your own journey, you will find hope, consolation, intrigue and even laughter which will lead you to freedom.

Sandra Niche

Foreword

Overcoming is about bringing to light the effect that domestic violence and bullying has on not only the individual but the family at large. The emotional, physical and psychological effect that the individual experiences can be damaging to the individual.

Overcoming is a self-help book that helps the reader to come to terms not only with the behaviour of the perpetrator but highlights tips for anyone to be able to identify the signs of abuse.

In one of the chapters, the writer talks about how she had to fight back in order to survive the attack of the perpetrator against her. She also talks about how she was raised in an environment where the rule was 'children should be seen and not heard'.

Does this come from the view held by her parents who are out of touch with the needs of their children, not listening not bothering to take time to respond to their emotional needs as they make the transition from childhood through adulthood.

INTRODUCTION

It is only through the divine intervention of the Holy Spirit that the contents of these pages have come into being. I have experienced many miracles in my life, and I hope that the reader will be enlightened to go from strength to strength whilst journeying through the pages of my book.

I have been through some tough times; finding it harder to explain in ordinary words of the problematic situations I encountered but through the Divine strength God endowed upon me I managed to survive. As I put pen to paper, my only resolution to the unanswered questions I had, and to bring relief to what I was experiencing, was to produce a book.

I hope somewhere in these pages someone will connect with my story which will comfort them, that whatever they are going through they can rise above it, if they believe in themselves.

CONTENTS

CHAPTER 1

QUAGMIRE OF A LONESOME LIFE

I was born into a family of nine children, with five brothers and three sisters. I was the eldest of the girls. I was born in Kingston, the capital of Jamaica and then moved to St Catherine when I was six years old. I lived with my parents until I was seventeen.

Dad had a fairly good job; he left for work early mornings and came home late at nights. I used to wait for him to come home from work, regardless of how late it may be. Dad worked as an ordinary postman until the company he worked for upgraded his job to a private contractor, which made it more secure.

As a child, I always wanted that emotional and physical support from my parents, which they failed to give me. I think they were busy with the expense of keeping a family, especially my dad. My mum didn't work because she had the responsibility of looking after my younger siblings.

I grew up in an environment where domestic violence was present and that always made me feel unsafe. Dad used to stay busy with his work schedule while Mum was busy with hers.

I used to feel neglected; I guess that's what happens when a family is large, and the smaller ones get all the attention. Sometimes children can feel left out. Sometimes I needed my parents to sit and talk with me regarding issues I was experiencing, but unfortunately that never happened. I do think they had good intentions, but it was the demands of the family which caused us to feel that way.

I was not able to share my feelings with my other siblings about the abuse that was happening around us because they too were experiencing the same thing. We were all accustomed to that lifestyle and just got on with it. Just the sound of Dad's thundering voice would make me become fearful. Whenever he started, he would call Mum names like "you foolish woman, who can't even help". How could Mum go out to work when she had children to look after.

I never forget she told me she used to work at a dry cleaner and one day she got ready for work but because she did not have anyone to look after me, she resigned. I empathise with my mum and appreciate the sacrifice she made for me. Therefore, I felt obliged to help her.

It is when I became an adult and started having children, I realise the sacrifice parents make for children. I came to understand now why some families experience domestic violence; it can be because of financial reasons whereby one party is feeling the strain of the responsibility of the family. However, to alleviate the stress and reduce violence within the home, families need to have regular dialogue and address the problems rather than ignore them.

I am not trying to find an excuse for my dad's behaviour, but it's reality. Especially if the stress has not been addressed properly through communication.

Is not only my family that experienced domestic violence, it is a worldwide problem. So, I am not trying to embarrass my dad but making a point and addressing an issue. There are a lot of relationships from different cultures that experience domestic violence.

People who find themselves in an abusive relationship can experience it emotionally, physically, or psychologically. So, my reason for writing on this level is that I am trying to reach not only Jamaican men but men from all cultures, women too. Domestic violence is an epidemic throughout all nations, and it should be a concern for all.

Also, families are being destroyed because people are scared to talk about what they are experiencing. I believe the reason for that is that people are made to feel ashamed that they maybe disgracing their families.

After I wrote my first edition of *Survivor*, I was attacked by one Ava Brown an author, saying how I have embarrassed my family.

It's our people that are trying to bring us down; we shouldn't be made afraid to talk about what is bothering us. We should be uniting to combat against domestic violence rather than trying to intimidate people who are speaking against it.

So, to avoid being targeted, ridiculed and ostracised from their families; people shun the topic and suffer in silence.

Globally, domestic violence is on the rise. I have looked at the statistics of domestic violence in Jamaica and according to source "One in four women in Jamaica experience intimate partner violence," reveals the first national surveys' Women's Regional Director for America and the Caribbean, Luiza Carvilho, who drew the attention of closing the data gap on violence against women. According to source "there's an absence of reliable data and therefore it is not possible to treat adequately, reduce or prevent violence against women." This is to show the scale of how domestic violence is escalating and has reached a stage where it has become difficult to manage. www.unwomen.org

In Britain, the latest figures (released on 22 Nov 2018) from the Crime Survey for England and Wales show little change in the prevalence of domestic abuse in recent years. In the year ending March 2018, an estimated 2.0 million adults aged 16 to 59 years experienced domestic abuse in the last year (1.3 million women, 695,000 men). Domestic abuse in England, https://www.ons.gov.uk .

Looking at these figures, it is obvious that we have a worldwide problem and need to try new interventions to see if we can at least reduce the figures to a more manageable level.

Referring to a YouTube video; whereby a news presenter along with a Criminal Lawyer visited the San Francisco County Jail to conduct an interview with the perpetrators of domestic violence. This is to view the issues that affects these men and to find out why they are violent and how best to help them.

Also, they invited a Facilitator from the domestic Violence Programme Restorative of Justice, who works with Resolve an organisation to stop the violence in relationships. She shared her story how she was abused by her husband, hoping it will help the men to see where they have gone wrong.

Also, to see how they can be helped and to reduce the violence, especially for those who are incarcerated by letting them take responsibility for their action. She feels that by them listening to the recording of what happened to her, these men would feel remorseful and turn from being violent.

One of the perpetrators talked about moments when he apprehended his victim. Firstly, to objectify the victim with what he calls "Chin checking". This is when the victim would suddenly realise they have been hit on the chin. Then followed by a slap, which would then escalate into more violence. Many women find themselves in these circumstances, then the perpetrator would vow not to do it again. Unfortunately, that one time turns into years of abuse.

Jackie spoke about moments of how her husband would try to reduce her self-esteem daily, by undermining her. Saying, she is nothing and cannot live without him. Then the abuse would escalate from mental then emotional and psychological. This she claimed has damaged her self-esteem over the years.

This is some of the abuse Mum went through. Unfortunately, I never heard her mention any of this, she seemed to have accepted it. I think if she had spoken about it then we girls wouldn't have experienced it.

Growing up, I never saw that my mum worked, she was always at home looking after us, which is a full-time job. Dad was the one who worked. I do think if he knew how to get Mum involved in his work maybe she could work alongside him and rotate their working hours. That would have made life easier.

Men need to realise that women need support and to feel appreciated. Especially when they are left at home to look after the family.

However, things are not as they were a few years ago because times have changed, and women are more independent and know how to balance family and work. They are becoming more empowered and ambitious where they occupy careers that were once considered male orientated.

As a child, when growing up and witnessing Dad being upset with Mum it wasn't just emotional for me, it affected me psychologically too. The physical attacks on Mum were a concern for me and left me feeling worried. It was frightening to see such action displayed and it made me develop fear.

Even though Mum was experiencing domestic violence in her relationship, I don't think she thought having more children wasn't a good idea. Instead, she found herself pregnant every year. That must have been hard and placed a lot of stress on her, both physical and emotional.

I noticed she never had the kind of support that some families had from their loved ones, like sisters and even her mum. I remember she used to take us to Grandma but never remember that she came to visit; it was we who visited her. That seemed rather selfish. Mum had to learn to cope on her own.

Looking back at the difficulties Mum endured, maybe if she had the awareness and education that is available today to other families in developed countries such as Britain, she would've been able to plan her family better.

As the eldest girl, I had to bear some of the responsibilities for the younger ones. In my childhood I had seen many ups and downs, and for that reason I always gave value to money. I used to help my mother with all sorts of household chores, like washing and cleaning.

I remember going to the market and seeing individual women of all ages displaying their products. My brother and I would argue how to spend the money and what to buy. For example, if the person was elderly, he wouldn't want to buy from them. Even if the price was cheaper, he would rather buy from a younger person. Maybe he didn't understand back then. He has changed now, because he grew to understand the value of money. He is also a parent and has realised that saving money is vital.

I was forced to grow up fast because my siblings were much younger, and I had to help look after them. The inner turmoil and stress of everyday life was strenuous because I was worried about Mum and what she was going through at the time. However, I maintained a positive outlook towards life, even though at times I felt the pressure and felt like my childhood had been seized from me.

Before a larger house was built, my siblings and I had to share a room. However, the company was great, because we played and joked at night before bedtime. At times, our feet would end up in one another's faces, which was so funny to us as children.

I recall my older brother feeling disgusted at one of our brother's snoring because it disturbed his sleep. One night he decided to pull a stunt on him. He rolled a piece of paper, lit it and placed it at the corner of his mouth. We stood and watched it burn until it caught his lip… that night I can't forget. It may have seemed like a joke, but it was dangerous. These are all the silly things children do when they don't understand the dangers of their actions. Even though life was challenging, we still had good times and memories as children.

My bigger brothers were always eager to learn to drive, but Dad never made time to put them behind the wheel. However, with their keenness to learn, they were always finding opportunities to jump behind the wheel whenever Dad wasn't around.

On one occasion, my bigger brother decided to take the van for a drive, but unfortunately it ended up in the house. Luckily it didn't do much damage. I don't remember whether they were punished for their actions.

When speaking about some of the difficulties that I experienced as a child, some may think that I did not find time to have fun. However, my siblings and I created many happy moments. For example, I used to run behind my brothers, especially when they were going to the mango bushes. They used to call me "Sister" as a pet name. I asked my mum why I was called Sister, and she told me that when I was born, my older brother looked at me, saying, "That's my sister," and from that day the name stuck.

Growing up as children in a large family, our parents did not find time to take us to activities such as piano lessons or dance classes, but our schools used to offer them. For example, I was a member of the folk-dance group at my primary school.

As part of our culture, one of my duties as a child was to assist with the younger ones. Some children would think that this is unfair and that they are giving up their childhood. If we felt that our parents were being unfair, we would have to keep it to ourselves as in other cultures too, children are expected to help with the younger ones.

I mentioned that I used to follow my bigger brothers around. I loved going with them to the mango fields that had lots of mango trees. People would take the journey either by car, truck or simply walk to pick mangoes for free.

The mango bushes were quite a distance from where we lived. The journey was down a long, sunny and dusty road; tiresome to walk, especially if you wanted to find nice juicy mangoes.

I remember we lived in a lane, a narrow road with houses on both sides. My brothers and I would go out on the road and wait for trucks going to where the mangoes were. In our country we called it 'hopping trucks'. My brothers would run behind the truck, hold on and make sure they got into the truck, then call out to me to grab hold of their hand. They would pull me into the truck. Boy, wasn't that fun! We went from one extreme to the other. I was like a tomboy, behaving like a boy, doing things boys do.

As children, we would stuff juice boxes with paper, turn it into a ball and play 'Dandy Shandi'. It's a game with two people standing opposite to each other, at a distance, and someone in the middle. Someone would throw the ball to the person in the middle, but the aim of the game is not to let it catch you, otherwise you are out and someone else takes your place.

My brothers used to play cricket, too. They would use two pieces of zinc with a pole behind, to be the wicket. If the bowler hit the zinc when they threw the ball, the batsman was disqualified, and it was the next person's turn to bat.

I used to enjoy playing those games with them and with other children too. Another one was to ride on carts. My brothers would make the cart from pieces of board and four wheels that they found. They used to take me to this place in the community called Green Acre. The road was steep, and we would take turns to sit on the board and push each other.

To prevent accidents, one of my brothers would go to the bottom of the hill and make sure no vehicles were coming. The other brother would then set the cart off, or I would push it and watch. It sailed fast! The only thing to stop it was a wall where a wealthy family lived. We always admired that house. It was a huge house, and it had a beautiful garden. It was a sight to view.

I could say we were living dangerously, but we enjoyed it, including the fruit trees along the road where we played. We would throw stones at them to knock off the fruits, such as tamarinds in their brown shells, which you must break to suck out the flesh and then spit out the seed.

Another favourite was hog plum. Mangoes, cherries, guava, passion fruit, cashew fruits; we could easily find these in our community. Also, how could I have forgotten the common native dish of ackee, cooked with salt fish, roasted breadfruit, and fried plantain. Reflecting, these moments helped me keep sane.

As the family got bigger, the home environment became more intense. I guess the pressure of the growing family took a toll on my dad and he became aggressive and would lose his temper easily. I think he must have had a lot going on. Could it have been financial pressure?

I never understood what my parents had to endure whilst growing up, until I became a parent. That was when I realised how difficult it is to bring up children, especially when you are doing it alone or there is only one parent working.

We didn't have many friends that we could go to; or use their homes as a refuge. So, I had to learn to bear the stress of what I was experiencing. Also, I remember I used to be shy and felt insecure, maybe it's the problem that helped to contribute to my condition. As time went by, I realised lacking in self-confidence to approach people or make many friends was a big issue for me. In addition to the stress of dealing with my family issues and not sharing it with a friend, Dad wasn't the kind of parent who was keen on his children becoming too friendly with other children. So, the opportunity to want to confide in someone wasn't available. Also, I thought it was a private matter and just accepted what was happening.

Not all parents understand that domestic violence can affect children in many ways, including mentally, emotionally and psychologically. No one is perfect; and there's no family that can say they haven't had days when things go wrong, but it's knowing how to manage the difficulties is what matters.

When we are affected by issues such as domestic violence and it affects us deeply, it is only God that can heal our soul and emotions from those traumas.

Dad used to tell us not to go to people's houses because they would give us food that was not good. Talking about not eating from people, I have an aunt whose best friend poisoned her with an orange.

She was a teacher, and I am not sure if her friend was jealous of her. Sometimes we can have friends that are jealous and may think to do us evil. So, it's good to be cautious of who we eat from. We never know who will harm us. I do think all parents have a way of protecting their children.

I did feel unloved many times by what was happening with my parents, by them not stopping to think how what was happening was affecting me. The disagreements created emotional disturbance within me, causing anxiety of not knowing what might happen.

As a child, I used to look forward to my birthdays but, unfortunately, I do not remember having birthday parties because my parents were busy paying attention to other stuff.

However, I am not angry at them at this moment because since

I became an adult, I came to realise how difficult it is sometimes to balance a family. Though I try to remember my children's birthdays, because that is important to them.

However, Dad used to buy me little white dolls, that looked like princesses with crowns on their head, I never forget.

I know somewhere in his heart there was good because there were odd times when Dad would share jokes which made us laugh; to be consistent was hard for him.

Not everyone will understand, especially if their upbringing was different. I still love my dad, even though he made mistakes and was harsh with me on many occasions. I have come to a realise that people can't give what they don't have. Maybe he wasn't taught how to love, so it was hard for him to show us love.

Also, if parents are overloaded with issues of life and the responsibilities seem great, it can cause them to stress, especially if it is only one person working.

With me and my children alone as a single mother, it could be challenging and that has opened my eyes to what my dad might have been going through.

Also, I came to learn what might be the core reason for disagreements within the home which was that dad wasn't getting the right kind of support from Mum. According to him, he had tried hard to provide for us children and that Mum wasn't supportive of him and what he was doing.

I was young, so I didn't understand what exactly he meant. All I know is that as a child I should be looking forward to birthdays and having fun.

Raising children is a job on its own, especially in third world countries where parents do not get subsidies from the government. It can be difficult. I think the law needs to change in some countries, like Jamaica, especially when it comes to education, to make it easier for children to be educated. Especially for struggling families.

Writing this book wasn't easy, but I need parents to understand that the home environment is important for children to thrive and have a healthy life. It is disturbing for children to see violence displayed before their eyes. It can be damaging for them and affect them mentally, psychologically, and emotionally.

Also, domestic violence can make the child feel disconnected from parents. For example, it would be difficult for children to communicate their feelings and feel safe. We felt that our parents were not aware of the emotional or psychological effects that domestic violence had on us children.

Poverty can be a contributing factor to domestic violence, as well as a lack of education. I do believe, if government put extra resources in place to educate the public more about domestic violence, it could reduce the number of tragic deaths. This topic should be part of the curriculum in schools whereby children are made more aware of the subject matter.

I feel in less extreme cases where domestic violence is detected, the offence shouldn't be criminalised, but the offender be put on programmes that can help them to identify their problem and work with them to overcome.

Domestic violence is an epidemic, and it is on a rise within society. Domestic violence affects every nation, both the developing and the developed countries.

Dad was very strict and never failed to administer the strap at any cost. If we stepped out of line, then we would be sure we would pay the price for our wrongdoing. I guess that was how he was brought up and he didn't know any better. It is not easy to be correcting a child over the same thing continuously, but slapping does not solve any problem. Parents sometimes need help how to deal with difficult situations and how to solve problems without resorting to violence.

As a child I have witnessed too much and wish my parents had had a better way to resolve their problems. I am a believer that people should separate if they find themselves fighting, especially if children are involved. Protecting children is important.

People need to take responsibility for their actions and not blame others. I can honestly say I did see some of my dad's traits within me when I started having children, such as being strict.

I am not saying we ought not to be firm with our children. Every parent has standards and children need to know the boundaries but is how we approach the situation that is important.

I have learnt, there are other ways to approach life than being too strict. It doesn't make things easier, especially in this time.

Children are becoming more challenging, and parents are often not able to keep up with discipline. Or maybe they are resorting to the same method their parents used to bring them up; but it is not working. This is causing frustration within families. I don't think many parents deliberately want to hurt their children.

However, because the skills they are using to bring up their children are not working, they become frustrated and resort to violence which is not helpful.

Teenagers exerting violence upon parents

It has been impressed upon me to draw the attention about domestic violence from another perspective, children and teenagers becoming violent towards parents. It has been on different social media such as YouTube whereby the level of violence coming from teenagers, both boys and girls, towards parents which even ends in fatality is on the rise.

BBC News report: Domestic Violence: Child-parent abuse double in three years. According to source "The number of reported crimes involving children attacking parents has doubled in the past three years, data suggests with the highest percentage in Lincolnshire and West Midlands second. BBC.co.uk-Domestic Violence

Comparable data for 19 police forces in England, Wales and Channel Island saw annual incidents jump from 7,224 in 2015 to 14,133 in 2018. A charity said, "Violence towards parents could indicate a cry for help, with support "often too hard to access."

The issue surrounding this topic focuses on intimate partners, but I do feel the same amount of emphasis should be focussed on teenagers just as for men who beat their wives. This is to try and put a stop to these behaviours to try and reduce domestic violence in grown men. These youths are the ones that becomes husbands and partners and violent towards their wives.

Review Criminalising Youths

Instead of criminalising the youths, the government should put an infrastructure in place like Boot Camp, a place of rehabilitation that teenagers go to other than prison. This is for them to be there for few months before being sent home under strict order. That place should have a classroom environment where they learn life skills and teach them values and how to conduct themselves because many of these youths are from single parent homes, fathers are absent. In that environment that means they are keeping up with their schoolwork and learning some skills and not missing out on their education.

After the prescribed period they are serving comes to an end, then their behaviour tested through an exam and if they pass the test then they should be granted release. They should be sent home with strict orders to follow and if they violate them, then they should be re-admitted for double the time they were there until they learn.

The police force needs to review how they deal with issues, especially when it comes to families and be more sensitive towards citizens and work with parents who are challenged by their children without criminalising them. Many youths have potential, but sometimes haven't got good father figures to nurture them because they have not been around them and that's why they go astray.

Our youths are the future and the government need to put more money into community organisations to help keep young people in line with activities they enjoy. Also, these young people need to learn more skills which can be profitable for them and to help them focus. Young people are bored in the home, that is why they turn to violence because they haven't got anywhere to exert that extra energy.

Another factor I believe that causes this rise in violent behaviour from young people towards parents is; the government has taken the control of discipline out of the hands of parents and children are using that against parents. I am calling for the government to review their policy around disciplining children and give parents more control whilst they are not abusing the children and if the discipline has been done reasonably well.

According to KATHLENE M. HEIDIE from University South Florida: "Murder in the family, although shocking and unsettling, is not uncommon". According to her, the public has been analysed, and the national homicide data made available which revealed that, when the relationships between victims and offenders were known, one of four murder victims was slain by members of his or her own family during the period 1977–1986. According to her, approximately 1 out of 11 of these family members involved parents who had been killed by their children (HEIDIE 1989) Journal of interpersonal violence, vol 8 No.4, December 1993 531-544 1993 Sage Publication, Inc.

I think if parents form small groups so that they can meet up and share their problems and suggest solutions, it might help to reduce the frustration many are experiencing. Domestic violence within the home can cause children to become fearful.

When I was a child and saw what was happening around me, I would wonder when it would end. It was when my eldest brother got older, he put a stop to the violence. He began to defend Mum whenever a situation got out of line.

There is a song that says, "Children live what they learn." This is not to say children haven't got the potential to do good and make better choices, when they've realised there is much to achieve when one makes good choices.

CHAPTER 2

Hell, ON THE INSIDE HELL ON THE OUTSIDE

Living in an environment where there is constant quarrelling and fighting, whether from one's parents or siblings, can be frustrating for anyone. Domestic violence was something I saw as a child and never knew it could have a negative effect on the individual or for the children. I don't think my parents had any idea how damaging this was for us children.

Going to school, I thought was a way of escape from the hostile environment, until I started to experience bullying from a girl from my community. She would harass me whenever she got the chance. At the time I was eleven years old approaching twelve, about to finish Primary School. I was very slim and of a quiet nature.

Maybe because of my size she thought I was an easy pick for her to bully. Maybe this girl had the experience of being bullied which is why she bullied me.

Going to school was a worry for me because I wasn't sure when I would be attacked. I was happy to be able to go to school because it was an escape from the memory of seeing the display of domestic violence, especially when an argument developed between my parents.

I don't remember my parents having any idea of what was happening to me. In fact, I used to hide in the toilet to avoid going to school. However, that didn't last because I didn't have any option other than to go and face my giant. Also, there were certain activities in school that I was part of, like the folk-dance group. I enjoyed being part of the performance for my school and wasn't going to let the bully steal that from me.

Sometimes when I thought of how this girl used to torment me, I wondered if she had problems – why she tried so hard to make me unhappy. During that time experiencing bullying, I don't remember my parents having a clue what was happening to me. I realised I was becoming withdrawn from socialising, not wanting to go to birthday parties or hang out with my friends. I think because of what was happening to me, it started to affect my self-esteem.

How I came to realise the problem was affecting me; I was invited to a birthday party and during the gathering when everyone was enjoying themselves, I felt sad, so I walked away. What was the reason? I don't really know. Looking back, that seemed odd, but I never thought that bullying could affect the victim so deeply.

There were days when I felt like I didn't want to go to school, but my education was important, and I had to become resilient not to let the circumstances destroy my future. To be honest even if I had told my parents what was happening, they wouldn't be concerned because they had their own problems.

However, I was glad I had my older brother looking after me, so he intervened. One day whilst he was waiting for me after school, he noticed the girl was about to give me my daily walloping. He shouted at me and headed straight towards a heap of gravel which was on the school compound and threw some at her. You should have seen her running like lightning. She realised my brother wasn't joking and surely wasn't a pushover.

I had a break from her harassment and that was a relief. It felt like a breath of fresh air. I was enjoying myself going to school, believing this girl gave up her antics until suddenly, she started again and changed her course of attack.

In My Own Home She Came to Beat Me

Once a bully, twice a bully. Their ambition is to overpower and subdue their victim to control them. I must make it clear I am not glorifying violence, I did not know any better at the time, so my action was the only way I knew how to solve this problem.

This time it was in my home when she came trying to intimidate me. I realised this was a battle I had to win. Like David and Goliath. I saw myself as David; small with hidden strength and she, likened unto Goliath; big and strong. She had broad shoulders, a big bust and was stockily built. I realised she was calling me names like "skinny and wingy".

This was because I was slim built. I tried to ignore her at first, thinking to myself this isn't real. I said to myself "In my own home she came to bully me?" This was the last straw, and I was ready to do something about it. When she realised verbally abusing me wasn't getting anywhere, she started throwing stones.

I thought this was going too far and today was the day to fell this Goliath. Can you imagine "wingy and skinny" going to challenge "fatty"? Oh God; fear mingled with courage. I wasn't going to lose this battle, So, I embraced courage and acted.

Action Time

There comes a time when we must take the matter in our own hands; this is my opinion. Not everyone will agree.

I climbed down from my almond tree, not knowing what would happen. She was staring at me, and I was outstaring her. I felt intimidated by her size; something was telling me she was going to tear me to pieces.

Is she going to defeat me, the thought came to my mind? These thoughts were floating around in my head because of her size but

I knew that this day was the day to put an end to the years of misery and it wasn't my brother who was going to do it, but me.

Standing before her, boy wasn't that scary? My heart started pumping, goosebumps and cold sweat started to wash over my whole body. I grabbed her hair; courage took over and suddenly we were all over each other until an old lady came and pulled us apart, saying "Go home to your parents." That was the last time she ever bullied me.

CHAPTER 3

PARENTS LACK VISION FOR THEIR CHILDREN

Every parent's responsibility is to ensure their children's future is secure, to give them a good education. No child should be left to struggle their way through life.

At sixteen and advancing in grades, my teachers thought I had the potential to do well academically. So, they decided to ask for the presence of my parents to discuss my future. Dad was the one working and I was expecting him to take the lead. I was too timid to say this to him, knowing what he was like. Also, I already knew the answer he would give (*i.e. he must go to work and wouldn't be prepared to lose a day's pay*). This is what he told all of us from day one, so his stubbornness and refusal to support us educationally led to our downfall. Our future was taken away from us because we had parents who never cared enough to sacrifice so that we could achieve. All the teachers wanted to know from Dad was, what financial assistance would he be prepared to give to get me extra help to prepare for the CXC examination.

My question is; where was Mum in all this? One may ask. Mum wasn't strong enough to challenge Dad where his responsibility was concerned. She was powerless, not willing to fight for us children. So, we were left to suffer at the hands of our hard father.

Even though she wasn't the breadwinner, at least the effort would have counted. Her lack of ability could well be from her upbringing. Or maybe she didn't think she could have persuaded my dad because she wasn't earning.

So, she thought she didn't have a say where the spending of the money was concerned. They were lacking in vision where us children were concerned. Such was the cruelty of my father's regime. Parents should understand that when they start having children it's all about sacrifice.

Speaking about my parents not showing concern or getting involved in my education or anything that concerned me, I remember being part of the Friendship Primary School Folk Dance group and used to enter competitions. Not having any of my parents present was very disappointing for me. This made me feel left out, abandon, and rejected.

This time Dad could be forgiven, because I didn't expect him to stop from work to come and watch me representing my school. Mum could have shown some effort by giving me moral support, but she never showed up. To be honest, I am not sure if she knew I was involved in school activities.

Going back to my education, I had only one chance left where exams were concerned, that was the Secondary School Exam, so I made good use of it. I never forget how Dad would send me to school without lunch money or the taxi fare, making it clear he hadn't got any money. Yet he would secretly ensure one of my younger sister's daily expenditures was met. This, although instilling feelings of rejection, made me more determined to push towards my goal. It was my good friend who gave me money for the taxi fare and lunch money. I never forget her kindness.

Graduation Day was fast approaching, and this was the day every parent would want to make memorable for their child or children. Sadly, I didn't hold out much hope for parental involvement, except for making it known that I needed a special dress for the occasion.

Whatever made Dad decide to ask his sister in America, Aunt Eunice, to send a dress left me baffled. Incidentally when the parcel arrived it was the ugliest white lace frock I had ever seen in my life!

When I asked for a belt to make the dress look nicer, he roared: "Everything you see people with, you want!" Wow! What more could I ask for? Mind you, a good neighbour stepped in to ensure I had a belt for the big day. Speaking of Graduation Day, when most parents were crammed into every inch of space outside and inside just to catch a glimpse of their loved ones and cameras were flashing, I didn't have the presence of either of my parents there. This made me feel like they did not care.

Life After Graduation

All individuals that leave school have hope, dreams and aspiration; they just need someone's support for them to achieve.

The only jewels in the crown to hang on to, was the results of three subjects from the SSC exams which made my teachers and I proud. I tried to make use of what I had by applying for a course at Papine College in Jamaica, to study to become a Dietician. This was because I got the highest level in Catering. Unfortunately, after some time waiting for a response, I was told they couldn't find the certificate. That had left me feeling confused. If I had someone to give me career advice then, I maybe would have been able to try and retrieve the certificate that got misplaced and pursue my dream.

It was after leaving school that reality hit me. I started to feel lonely. However bad my experience was regarding being bullied; I missed the odd days with my friends. Can one imagine how difficult it must have been for me coming from a home whereby parents never cared, and I had to face life alone? However, it made me develop resilience.

There were times I felt lost and lonely. I was a shy girl who was unable to look people in the eye without feeling awkward. Looking back, I think bullying may have contributed to the shyness. Also, the experience of domestic violence because that can affect one mentally, emotionally, and psychologically.

Even though I was able to secure the basic qualifications, I did my best and was determined to fend for myself. As I got older, I noticed something start happening to me which I couldn't explain – fear deeply embedded in me yet counterbalanced by a feeling of optimism which was hard to explain. It was like even though I was experiencing some negative feelings such as fear, I was determined to push past those barriers.

I was feeling psychologically entrapped. It was like trying to free myself from that feeling so deeply rooted. This feeling started escalating over months and years which caused me to lock myself indoors, not wanting to be around anyone. I couldn't explain to anyone that I was either depressed or experiencing mental health illness. I wish I'd had the privilege to get help to sort out my mental health. In Britain there is help accessible for people who go through domestic violence.

Not wanting to be around people wasn't something that seemed abnormal to me. I thought I was just going through a phase. Whenever I was alone and heard voices or footsteps, just the slightest movements would trigger a quiver of tension within me. This was even worse if it was someone with whom I was familiar. I think that emotion was a feeling like someone is going to hurt me and it stems from my experience of the domestic violence I saw as a child.

I started noticing a slight change within my complexion. As I drew near the mirror to take a closer look at myself, I noticed my entire features had changed to dark brown, given I am fair in complexion.

This was a sign that I was ill, and no one knew, not even my parents. I guess they were too busy arguing and fussing and fighting! I was experiencing tightness within my body. I knew something was wrong because I was losing weight and started suffering from chronic influx of acid. I never forget, the doctor sent me for a test whereby they inserted a camera down my throat. That was an awful experience.

Nothing they gave me solved the problem. It reached a stage where the condition worsened whereby my food wasn't being digested. That made me start losing weight rapidly. I thought I was going to die.

CHAPTER 4

CHURCH

What of spiritual support? It must be a reason why people join groups. Everyone has their own personal reason why they become part of something; for me it is my faith. I think the Church should be there to support any individual in every possible way they can. If they are unable to do anything, they should be able to direct the person to where help can be found.

Finding myself a new skill or becoming part of a social group I thought may just be the answer to the problem I was experiencing. Sometime or another in an individual life, people may find themselves on a journey and need support. In my quest to get more out of life and looking for a way out of the darkness I was experiencing, church was my answer.

I am not preaching; I am just telling my story. Everyone has their way of managing their problem. I did not have any other option because in Jamaica culture and tradition is what people follow. In more developed countries you can find diverse groups that have different ways to help others.

I wasn't aware of counsellors or psychotherapists, so I settled for what I was told works. In my own opinion if it works. Yes, I believe what a person believes in can either cure or hurt. All the issues we experience are because of traditions. If it's not our parents, it's society. There are norms that people are expected to follow. Some work, others don't. People do not easily adapt to change, and change is not easily embraced.

Mankind doesn't generally like to try new things. I realised that the problems I saw within my family, were generational, and no one spoke about it, so it continues within the generation and, sadly, it destroys a lot of us. I am willing to address the issue and is not because I am exposing my family but is to bring healing and restoration to my generation. I found out even with me, some of the things I learnt as a child are so deeply embedded and it's not easy to change the way I think. I must be willing to unlearn the bad habits and replace them with good ones.

I don't want to see my children come and adopt this way of life because the regime is not profitable in terms of what is positive.

Becoming part of a faith group was something I had looked forward to because I wanted a place to pour out my distress and feel free. I was longing to feel happy and start to enjoy my life like other young people.

On a weekly basis, I sat in the congregation feeling nervous. I remember a Sunday morning when I was asked to read the Bible. Suddenly a feeling of fear swept over me, then I lost speech.

This thought popped into my mind, *"How are you going to face the audience?"* Somehow, I gained courage that I could do it and stepped forward even though I thought avoiding eye contact would be best for me.

As I began reading, I started crying. It wasn't that I couldn't read, it's just that thing that had a hold on me. This thing was determined to hold me captive so, yes that day was a disaster!

I had to examine my life and was determined to try another way to deal with this monster. For instance, I thought that becoming part of a social group would help me overcome these psychological barriers that present themselves in the form of fear and shyness.

I realised even though I was a person of faith, I was still affected by the feeling of fear and anxiety, but I held on to my faith knowing that I would be helped someday, because of my faith.

I think it was good for me to be introduced to the Church as I would need my faith to help me through the difficult times ahead.

Attending meetings and socialising with my peers had helped me to feel comfortable around people and re-gain self-confidence. Also, I learned to have a relationship with God by reading the word and believing.

CHAPTER 5

AUNT TOOK DISADVANTAGE

Whilst growing up, I thought our parents' responsibility was to take care of me to ensure that we children were protected; but this wasn't so with Dad. He left us to be abused by our Aunt Balda.

My dad came from a family of ten, and he was the eldest of his siblings. I am not sure what his upbringing was, because he never spoke about his childhood, except I could remember him saying that as a boy if he came home and found young smoke, the dinner just been cooked, he would be angry.

Both my sisters and I were sold out to out Aunty. She reminded me of the Cinderella story, except that my two parents were alive. We would be sent to her on weekends to wash and clean. Did Dad think Mum couldn't teach us girls how to do house chores? As a matter of fact, one of my younger brothers has a memory of this aunt's harsh regime.

As an Immigration Officer, she was able to hire helpers, but she was cruel and chose to put us through harsh treatment. Sometimes I wonder if it was because she had some vendetta against Mum.

I remember talking to Mum about her relationship with Dad's sisters. She said they weren't nice to her; especially Dad's big sister Eunice; that when she had her children, she wanted Mum to be the babysitter and because Mum did not comply as she had her children to look after, Aunt Eunice bore malice towards her. Why didn't Dad stand with Mum and support her? If he did, his sisters would have been more respectful of the family and treat us children better.

I can remember my cousin and three of my sisters that were used as Aunt Balda's housemaids because we were frequently sent there by Dad.

We were given the washing to do. For example, her white shirts. If the washing wasn't to her liking, it would be pulled from the washing line, thrown into the dirt and she would send us back to wash it all again.

The job for my younger sisters and I was to keep the house clean, making sure everywhere was tidied and the furniture spotless before Aunty came home. She used to hide the electric polisher and gave us the floor brush to kneel to shine the floor, upstairs and downstairs.

We used to live in fear and would stay up late listening out for her coming or, if we fell asleep, we ensured both upstairs and downstairs was tidy, and that no dust was left on the furniture or else we would be woken up and sent to re-do it – what a life we lived then!

Maybe the question is, why didn't we tell our parents? This aunty was wealthy and could afford certain things we weren't getting from our parents, so we loved going there for the nice little gifts. Aren't children vulnerable? As teenagers, we weren't aware that what was happening to us was child abuse. We thought it was the norm. I guess it isn't only in our family this sort of behaviour was portrayed, most Jamaicans could identify with my story.

What I am telling you is the truth. Dad told Aunt Balda that the only use my sister and I had was for her to use us. Was he going out of his mind? Or were the pressures of the family too much and she was a help to him financially that caused him to use such words?

I forgive him. See, I am not witch-hunting but bringing to the surface the things that affected me as a child and into adulthood. That they may well have contributed to some of my difficulties I experienced later in life.

Dad, along with his sister, had taken advantage of us. Abuse is a spirit that when it latches itself onto the individual, it causes difficulties throughout their life and only God can change the person's direction in life if they believe. "For the plans I have for you, is not to harm you, but to give you a future and an expected end." (Jerimiah 29 v 11)

One may find themselves being abused and not even aware of how it all started; maybe someone spoke something negative towards you which opens a door in the spirit world. This can cause negative vibes in one's life. "In the beginning, God spoke, and everything came into existence." (Genesis 1) As a child of God, I believe by faith and speaking positively one can counteract the negative.

I wrote this book not to embarrass my family but for parents' eyes to open; that through ignorance and wrong words spoken to our children, this can cause curses on them. Many times, we are guilty of not realising that some of the words used towards our children can have a negative affect on them.

Visited my second cousin, was this a good idea?

He was a single man, living with his two children and a nanny. I thought it would be safe for me since he had his children and his nanny living with him. Also, he was a preacher and I think preachers are respectable people who look after the needy.

I used to enjoy living there; his kids were lovely. Also, there was a bakery on the compound that baked buns, breads and patties. I helped some early mornings. He was kind and hardworking, I admired his strength to get up early and work hard to look after his children.

He baked breads, patties and cakes and delivered them to schools and shops. I used to admire his determination when he would wake up early in the morning and finish late at night. I used to help in the bakery too and it helped to instil good work ethics and values.

Things about to change

Sadly, things started to change; for example, I was his focus, and this was in the direction of a relationship which I would never dare go down that route. I respect my elders, especially preachers. I think they are sent by God to protect others; I guess that how it should be but not always. I was approached inappropriately, saying "cousin" and "cousin boil good soup".

Even though I was young and naive, I'm sure I wasn't any fool. So, I packed my things and went back home, not sure how to face Dad. I would hide and sleep under the bed because I didn't want him to see that I was back at home.

However, one day he came to realise I was in the house and gave me an ultimatum, saying "If you want to sleep with your younger sister, you have to pay a $150 for monthly rent," or if I wanted to rent a room in the house, the cost would be $450. I couldn't afford that amount of money, so I would hide under the bed several nights.

I couldn't bear this life for much longer, so I went to the Minister of my church to enquire if he knew of any Church member who could offer accommodation. So, I was told about this Church sister who was going to Canada for a few months and needed someone to look after her three children. Their ages were 17, 11 and 6 years old.

I embraced the opportunity which worked well for a while, until psychological problems developed with the 17-year-old who didn't wish to be spoken to by me. According to her, we weren't much older than each other. Also, she was complaining that she needed her bed and I was soon to be thinking how to move on. Whilst living with them, I met this guy whom I formed a relationship with, and this is how it began.

CHAPTER 6

MY FIRST LOVE

Every girl's dream is to marry her first love. When Roger first saw me, I could feel he loved me. He learnt of my circumstances and realised I was under pressure to move from where I was living. Also, he saw my need for emotional support and became protective, which made me feel he cared for me.

So, I decided to turn my attention to this young man because of the crucial time of my life and what I was experiencing – the need to move out from my Church sister's house.

That had left me with questions; for example, "Was this a prelude to my spiritual death?" Knowing full well that the surge of emotional needs was ever so strong within me, and the attraction between us was spontaneous and could lead me into sin. The nature of this relationship was such as to awaken my feelings, call it infatuation I suppose when I look back at the situation.

At that time, I was twenty-one and he, five years older. Roger was the ideal man of my dreams. This is not his real name but a made-up name. In terms of stature, he was five feet nine, carrying a good body weight of about sixteen stones, enough to earn himself the pet's name "bulk man". His eyes were big and bold; he was clean shaved, well dressed and well presented. Not only was he academically qualified but skilled in terms of a trade. He was an electrician. For want of family such as his, that seemed caring, I thought then they had good family values. He was the youngest of his siblings and lived with his parents. Roger was the first guy for me, and I really loved him.

Roger's attraction for me started back in my teenage years which I wasn't aware of until he approached me for a relationship when I was older, 21 years old, and he told me. Years after he did work for my dad on the new house during its building and that is how he came to know me. For me, his beady bold eyes had never failed to awaken my earliest responses to learn to value and respect his presence! So much so, as the years rolled over, a deep-seated and binding attraction was the product of love.

Psychological Conflict

This has to do with trying to balance Church and relationships, and think I could still maintain Godly principles; something had to give way and I compromised my faith, and this was when things went wrong.

I was torn between love for Roger and my faith which caused my mind not to be at peace. This was because spending quality time with Roger may well have caused me to fall. I realised the more we spent time together, the more we developed a need for each other.

I was always feeling that guilt when we were together. This was because my faith preaches, marriage before sex; and Roger was approaching life in the opposite way. Fear was mingled with love, and we couldn't help feeling strands of gratitude welling-up inside our body. It's the feeling of love that I didn't receive from home that came in a different form.

Even though I felt love, there were other thoughts that were constantly bombarding my mind. For example, what was I doing with an unsaved man? This was because I was a Christian. What is this doing for my status within the Church community?

At the time I was a member of a local church and living with a Church sister. What of my commitment to values upheld by the

Church? My difficulties in engaging Roger on any level of discussion to do with Bible or Religion was another source of worry could I get him to listen? No way, he'd just change the subject at random. So now I was torn with the decision to let go of this man and come clean, easier said than done!

Given that my childhood years had been besieged by a catalogue of harsh treatments, why did a loving God allow such abuse to befall me? Day after day I wrestled with these thoughts because I wasn't willing to walk away from a man who gave me as much nurturing as to make me feel wanted and loved; after all Roger was my first love! It was hard for me to give him up just for the sake of conscience. As a Christian girl, I thought perhaps I should have had the good sense to balance both Church and love life. But then I was only fooling myself, because I had no experience out in the world. Roger was as stubborn as an ox, he wasn't going to walk with me on any Christian pathway, but love blinded the truth, I deceived myself. We saw each other at our most convenient time, because both of us used to work with the same community, so we had to schedule when it was convenient for each other.

The love and intimacy between us grew rapidly. After five months of relationship between us, I discovered I was pregnant. It was time to decide where I was going to live, providing I was still living at this Church sister's home. I started developing mixed emotions; the contributing factor arose from how the members of the Church would treat me, not to mention my parents who never cared in the first place. One night a message was sent to me by one of my siblings that my dad needed to see me urgently. I knew he heard that I was pregnant, and I was wondering why this was important to him, knowing the dad I had from a child, one that didn't care about anything that concerned me or my future, so why now?

That night I embraced hope and courage and went to see him. Roger was determined that nothing was going to change my mind from carrying his child, not even my own dad. He supported me at the meeting with my dad and mum who had nothing to say as she stood and listened to my dad giving me his sermon. All my dad did that night was to cast more guilt and he started to blame my mum that she put me up to this. What the hell was going on I asked myself. I thought to myself that he was so blind, self-righteous and full of denial that he was unable to see his fault as a dad. According to him, Mum should have been more vigilant, whilst he was out working, and prevented this from happening – as if I was living under his roof. This was even more confusing for me. Whilst he was working it was to maintain his own ambition which he failed to see.

He had forgotten that he was the one who threw me out at 17 and left me with no option. All I could hear that night as usual was blame, and my mum was the scapegoat. Roger and I didn't have any option that night other than to walk away because no moral support was in the making to offer to me, his daughter.

The feelings of confusion, happiness, guilt and thinking that I had betrayed Christ made me start feeling overwhelmed. Not considering that I am human and will fail wasn't a belief instilled within me from my faith, but rather condemnation. The impression that God is going to zap me out of this life because I transgressed his law laid heavily upon me. No thought of what Jesus has done on the cross, over two thousand years ago, was evident within me because I was filled with guilt.

Looking back at my life and seeing how God has been good to me has made me realise that it is not our own work, but it is the Grace of God. His love encompasses all my failure.

As this TV Evangelist said, why carry the guilt when Jesus takes care of it when he went to the cross; we only worry when we lack faith. The reason I felt guilty was because I didn't want to have my children before getting married. I was also thinking of the impact it would have on my faith and how I would be treated. God knows everything about us, even our failure.

My friend, when she found out I was pregnant, suggested to let her help me with the baby and separate myself from the dad. Maybe she was thinking long term that the relationship wasn't going to work and was trying to save me from the pain to come. However, at that stage of my life there was too much emotion floating around and even if the suggestion was good, I couldn't see it then.

Also, that was the most difficult decision to make because I believe the child has the right to know who their father is. Roger was overwhelmed with joy, bursting with happiness and feeling proud that at last the moment to become a dad was inevitable. He saw I was confused but to him he gave me all the support needed at the time. He knew I would need somewhere to call home and it was down to him to make it happen.

At the time he lived with his parents and thought it would be quicker to secure accommodation where he was. Also, it was important for him to see the developing stage of his child. This was one of the happiest moments I ever witnessed in his life.

At the time I felt all the confusion was about to come to an end and it was an honour to be invited to his home to meet his parents. Also, meeting the rest of his siblings whenever they visited was something I looked forward to. His other siblings lived abroad.

The friend I spoke about was my boss at the school where I was teaching. This had made me feel even more vulnerable in the sense that if I didn't comply with her suggestion, I may find myself out of work. My job was important to my independence, and I wouldn't want to find myself totally dependent on Roger. It instilled a freshness and newness of experience in the sense that it was the job satisfaction for money and material things.

Forgiven

During your most confusing state of your life, God is in it with you.

It was during those moments of uncertainty when a visiting Evangelist came to church. As I walked through the door, I thought it was safe to sit at the back because I was feeling fearful that she would say out loud that someone in the congregation was pregnant. She made a request that those who need prayers should come to the front, to be prayed for. Everyone who felt the need went up, except me! In my confused state, I heard her say "you at the back come here!"

My heart skipped a beat, but I had no option than to go up. Upon approaching her, she smiled at me. That caused me to feel at ease. She whispered, "You know what you have done, but God says to tell you, He has forgiven you!" That is the father's love that the Bible speaks about. God is love and he proved he loved me even when I failed him.

The love she demonstrated gave me the strength to face the adversity ahead. To be honest, there were some who showed me love, but the wife of one of my pastors looked at me with scorn. I never forget those whispering words of the preacher.

Web of deception

Anyone can be deceived. Each perpetrator has their own motive, and their aim is to achieve their goal, come what may.

Admitting my own limitations, I was beginning to see how foolish and naive I was. For all I cared, this was telling me how little I knew of the outside world let alone men. What do they want? As an innocent and trusting young woman (to the point of thinking all that glitters is not gold), I had to learn the hard way. Coming to the realisation that the whole thing was a trap, that the devil was setting me up and I was about to fall into that trap. By the time I was on the verge of getting out I was already drawn into the web. Stands to reason that Roger's amazing masculine frame, his bold bright eyes and his charm were just for a season – and the season was about to expire! Roger was the web, and I became the spider (hence, the moral of the story), i.e., once you fall into that web, God help you if you come out alive!

As the pregnancy progressed, Roger started to make suggestions; for example, he said to me one day that he had lost five children from a previous relationship. I enquired how come? According to Roger, it has to do with spirits. He claimed that each time the person got pregnant she was unable to carry them full term.

This story started to freak me out and I was starting to wonder what his conclusion was. To my surprise Roger suggested a bush bath. What was this? He added, "I have a man I want to take you to, he will bathe you so you and our baby can be protected from evil spirits." I have never ever thought of going down such a route. I was startled, confused and felt trapped. How can I get out of this, I asked myself?

That was a question nobody but me could answer and I didn't even have the answer. I was stuck and nobody could help because I was pregnant and couldn't face my family, I had no family to support me. I went with the idea and there Roger fulfilled his most ultimate desire and I am left with the battle to fight. After that bath, did I feel protected? No, I had feelings of guilt, confusion wrapped up with spiritual attacks and I felt like I was in hell. I was faced with spirits to fight; it was a battle before and after the birth of my baby.

Spiritual Death

Some may ask "What is this?" It's when someone who is a believer turns away from their faith, turns away from and loses connection with God but God never leaves them. It sounds confusing, no we don't leave God spiritually, fallen from grace. It is when he or she chooses to walk away from his or her faith and turns to something opposite to trust.

Spiritual death for me meant two things – walking away from my belief to hook up with a man who is completely outside the Church family and having conceived for him. In common-law terms this would be called 'living in sin', hence my question is, would he be prepared to come clean and offer to marry me?

This probably would have been a giant step to help alleviate my shame – not a chance! To be fair, there was marginal acceptance of his responsibilities whereby to purchase a house is concerned. He'd preferred to lodge within his parents' house. Roger wasn't thinking that that he needed to do what a man does – which is to take care of his family. The trade of an electrician was viable for him and gave him the security to provide.

The Birth of our Baby

When the baby was born, all seemed well with Roger, and he provided well. We weren't short of finance because I had worked up to my maternity leave, so we could provide the things we needed. We didn't need a babysitter because his parents and my sister helped.

Becoming a parent along with work commitment was a challenge, also taking care of the home. I had to learn to multi-task in order to balance everything around me. It was good that I had experience looking after my siblings, or else I wouldn't have been able to manage.

My sister and Roger's parents were a good help. Their support had helped me through the difficult stage of motherhood. Mum used to come around and offer a little support, but it was my siblings and the grandparents especially their grandfather, Roger's dad, who stood by me mostly.

As the relationship developed, I noticed Roger was becoming less interested in doing his part as a father. For example, bonding with the baby by spending time with her. Instead, he would find an excuse to disappear in the evenings after work.

It reached a stage in the relationship whereby Roger became lacking in interest where the upkeeping of the apartment was concerned. That is, not providing financially to buy the necessary things. I had to resume work early because I was feeling the strain of lack of finance to maintain our needs, such as clothing and shoes. Roger stopped providing.

It becomes a regular habit for him to stay out late during the week and on weekends too. He was so selfish not to realise that having a baby and balancing the home responsibilities and work was hard for me. He would be gone for hours leaving me to do the washing, cooking, and cleaning. It wasn't long before the relationship became difficult, and Roger became violent physically.

The stress was becoming too much, and I didn't have anyone other than my sister to share what I was going through. I wished Mum was more involved, but I did not have that kind of relationship that allows me to discuss such private issues, so I had to fight my way through.

There was something unusual with Roger disappearing, also my sister on a weekend. This started to look suspicious, but I was refusing to believe that anything out of the ordinary would be happening.

I thought she was just busy, as a young person, so I just got on with things. When Roger came home at nights after work, he would do anything to create an argument with me and then demand relationship.

He became a sexual controller, a head worker, trying to con me by telling me lies that he hadn't been to places when he knew he was lying. It wasn't long before I was pregnant again with baby number two. This is when I was plunged further into deeper confinement, abuse which led to more stress, but what could I do?

I was confused to what had happened to the man I'd met. Why suddenly had he turned out the way he did? I started to wonder if it was the responsibility of two children that brought on the stress. I had missed those wonderful moments we used to have when Roger and I walked home from work and spent quality times together.

I didn't experience the love I wanted from my parents, and Roger had shown me love when we first met which I had cherished. Those days he made me feel special had disappeared. Wanting to ask him what was wrong wasn't easy. This was because he became snappy and there wasn't any room to entertain a conversation that related to our future.

Every girl has that special image of the perfect partner, but life can offer the opposite. I think if Roger had good role models, he would have done well but it's the friends he had that led him astray. Also, if he was bent in his way, why should I blame his friends? He was a big man and should have taken responsibility for his actions.

Also, I think if we had shared the same belief, maybe we would have understood each other better. When I met Roger, he didn't seem aggressive, something must have happened along the way. Also, my question is; did we rush the friendship? After reflecting on the relationship and how things developed rapidly, I think we should have given ourselves more time to know each other. My advice to every young person who may come across this book is; give your relationship time to grow to know each other.

When Love Turns Sour

There are many reasons why relationships break down. For example, it may well be that people outgrow each other, but my question is; how can two people grow out of love with one another? I believe when people are truly in love, there are no ways they can outgrow one another. Love finds a way to make it work.

When I found out I was expecting my second child, I wanted more than just an ordinary relationship, I wanted commitment, but Roger wasn't thinking that way. Also, I had missed fellowshipping, Church, but the only way this was going to happen was if Roger would decide to come clean about whether he wanted to marry me or not. I remember he told me that during his teen years, he was actively involved in the Church.

I thought becoming a father was his ideal plan and family would be his priority. However, after I had my first child, I realised Roger wasn't heading in that direction. So, I had to plan what I was going to do with the rest of my life. This was because I didn't want to find myself just keeping on having children and never achieving my goal.

I decided, why should I let this man confuse me? He was the one who suggested the ritual to protect his child from evil spirits, according to him. I had no choice in the matter but to co-operate. So, following his instructions, I thought he would be prepared to stand firm and demonstrate his responsibility.

I remembered six months into the pregnancy something happened that arose suspicion in me. We were at home one evening, playing dominoes, my sister was there too. I realised it was getting dark, so I said to her to go home. He didn't seem pleased, but I stood my grounds. This was because she was younger than I and it was my duty to protect her, ensuring she reached home before it got dark.

When she left, Roger started an argument that she was his only friend, and I knew he never went out and how much I chose to interrupt his happy mood. I was a bit suspicious. However, I didn't want to jump to conclusions. So, I gave in to his manipulation and told him to go back for her. She was a girl that displayed humility and was very quiet, I guess simple. I wouldn't ever think my kids' dad was or would think of molesting my sibling, that was far from my mind.

Before he went for her, he started an argument and then became violent towards me. I humbly said, "Go back for her." One would ask; what was I thinking, telling him to go back for her. He got his heart's desire that evening.

A few months later we were blessed with the birth of our second baby girl. I thought Roger would be over the moon but no, the opposite! He seemed on edge, touchy as one might say; if a fly brushed past, he would erupt into cursing and swearing; at the impulse of light conversation, he was ready to lash out; before you knew it, I was on the receiving end when he became violent hitting on me.

I was trying to find the underlying cause for these mood swings. Like I've said, he was kind, gentle and loving right up to the birth of baby number one, but started to change gradually – why now was this sudden change? For instance, if he saw me talking to passers-by especially of the opposite sex, he'd be jealously assuming something was going on between us. With fights becoming common place, the onus was on me to defend myself. I wasn't going to stand and let this man beat upon me; I defended myself too, by throwing back punches. Anything I could find to hit him; I was determined not to take any nonsense from him.

When the situation seemed like it was getting out of hand, I remember asking Mum if she could assist me with child care which would free me up to get back into education, but she told me flatly no, that she had done enough to raise my siblings and wasn't prepared to do any more. In desperation, my 15-year-old sister was the one who volunteered to help.

The Truth Unveiled

This is just a lesson to anyone who reads this book and comes across this page, to know that you can't trust anyone a hundred percent. I am not saying you must start going around looking for signs from your siblings not to trust them.

Totally confused by his level of bullying, I instantly agreed, leaving a trail of unanswered questions: Was this man molesting my sister? She was my sibling, the only family support I had. Why was this man so concerned about my sibling's wellbeing?

From the dark corners of my mind, I quickly dismissed notions of a deep friendship developing between them. Suspicions burned deeply within my stomach, and I couldn't help searching his trousers' pocket, only to find a letter secretly in the inside pocket "You are mine" in my own sister's handwriting – this was when the penny dropped!!!

Betrayal – a double betrayal at that: How could a big man approaching his 30s stoop so low? What can a fifteen-year-old do for him? What was my sister thinking when she wrote such words? Right in my face! This left me so furious, and I thought, I had to challenge him. When I approached him, he was humble as a lamb, doing his best to assure me there was nothing going on between them. Did he take the letter she wrote him seriously? Moreover, he would never do anything to hurt me, he exclaimed.

How foolish was I to believe him, was I up for a challenge that would rip the union apart? I never thought so.

Tension escalated between me and Roger to the point where I decided my sister was no longer welcome at our home and if she did come, would have to leave early. As a matter of fact, according to Roger, his mother told him that when I was not at home she could come to the house. My question is "Did she love her grandchildren?"

I guess this didn't work because he planned alternative ways of hitting-it-off with her. For instance, pretending to be working every day especially weekends. Everything was in place; he knew very well where the love nest was going to be. Turning up late night after night, never without an excuse, took me to the point where I started disbelieving him again. I guess this didn't work because he planned alternative ways of meeting her. He had something up his sleeve. On that note, I thought ending the relationship for the children's sake and mine would be best – but how could I leave and where I would go?

Caught in the Very Act

I think I was too trusting and forgiving that I had forgotten to be cautious. Once bitten, twice shy. Once a thief, twice a thief. I'm not saying people can't change, but trust is earned.

For the reader of this page, let me take you back to the beginning of the chapter where I am identifying Roger's mood swing especially after the birth of our second child. Weeks leading up to the birth, he was doing his level best to balance a relationship between my sibling and me, hence, leaving him in an awful quagmire of guilt. To prove my point, I was admitted into hospital for several days to be treated for high blood pressure, and this is where he and my sister seized the opportunity to take control over my home. She, despite my orders not to stay late, was now sleeping over. Can you believe this?

Following the birth of my second daughter and immediate discharge from hospital, well past 8:00pm, she boldly offered to sleep-over to assist with childcare. While I was in the bedroom they were in the sitting room for hours. I didn't let that make me suspicious because the television was on. So, I thought they were just watching TV.

Shock-after-shock as I scrambled to the sitting room to have a quiet word with Roger. As I pushed my head through the curtain separating both rooms, I noticed she was in a lying position whilst his head was down in her face. Oh my God! This was the last straw in terms of ultimate betrayal – how could my own relative blood sister do this to me, hasn't she got any morals? "What's going on?" I asked. His face looked like a frightened child. That night I was convinced, the relationship was over.

As for my sister, she turned out to be a nasty piece of work. How evil can one be? Right in my face? Setting out to destroy the relationship between my children's father and me? Come to think of it, I remembered Roger making a prophecy to the effect of "I can turn your sibling's heart against you" – surely enough he succeeded in doing just that. One may ask, "Did your parents have any idea that their under-aged daughter had been molested by this man?" I told my mum. As a matter of fact, my sibling was always accosted by me. My mum was aware of how hurt and angry I was towards her. She always upheld my siblings in her wrong doings by attacking me.

That rose suspicion within me to why my mum hadn't given me the support I needed to protect my relationship. This wasn't just about me but for the children's sake. Mum blinded her eyes to what was happening to me and the children. Also, they were babies and needed their father. I think something suspicious was behind my mother's behaviour.

She was destroying a life I was trying to build with my children's dad. Nevertheless, he was just as guilty as her.

Tips to identify an abuser

1. Follows you around pretending to be protecting you.
2. He is always making you feel guilty or blames you for everything.
3. He tries to keep up with your whereabouts regularly.

4. He keeps track of your friendships.
5. He hits on you and keep apologising.
6. He blames you whenever things go wrong.
7. He tries to keep you away from your family.
8. He tries to keep you from working.
9. He is constantly belittling you.
10. When he hits you, he tells you it is your fault.
11. Withholding food, medication, or money?

CHAPTER 7

DECISION

No surrender; big fight. For all who read this chapter and is surprised. Remember when you give yourself to someone you sign a contract. You're saying to the individual that you have access to me any time; not everyone will agree. My faith teaches that; we must marry before intimacy. Sex outside of marriage is sinning against your own body.

There came a time in my life whereby I tired of living a life that was not profitable with Roger. So, I decided to turn my focus back to God. Many would think it's because things were not working out for me why I thought to go back in the Church. Maybe that could be the case. Also, once you have accepted Christ as your personal Saviour, you belong to him. He never lets you go, even when you've gone astray.

I was desperate to get back into fellowship, I told Roger.

"Come again?" he said.

I told him an Evangelist was coming to church and I would like to be there. That's how the conversation started. I asked him if he would be coming with me, surprisingly he said "Yes."

I had doubts about him joining me because he never kept his promises. That lying two-timer of a man, for a moment I never believed him. Anything to do with God, the Bible or Christianity, this man was as stubborn as an ox.

As I looked into his big, bold, beady eyes, part of me wanted to believe him. As for the rest, I wasn't wrong. The whole three-day event took place and no sign of him. Afterwards, bombarding me with excuses, i.e., "next-door neighbour took ill, and I had to rush him to the hospital," what a coincidence.

I told him I was recommitting my life to Christ and I would not be sleeping with him again unless he married me. Before the last word could come out of my mouth—

"You what?" grabbing me up, with his big voice filling up the whole room.

"You mean you won't be sleeping with me again?"

I said, "No." My heart started to beat fast, so the punches came one after the other. In no time he started slapping me right, left and centre. Returning thump-up-thump-up, I gave as good as I could. The big strong man started dragging me by my hair from his downstairs flat all the way upstairs to his parents' quarters.

His parents were crying out: "stop that now, now, now!" He was dishing-out more and more of his fiercest punches, and I was mashing-up his head with more thump-up thump-up!!! Old swine… thinking that Christians can't fight; he made a big mistake that day! The flesh was ready to fight back. That was my worst fight ever!

This man would be happy to tear me to pieces if he saw me trying to rise above his animal passions that sever humanity from divinity. Like a sexual predator, his one mission in life was to control and limit my movements. For him, his goal was to see me writhe in bondage beneath his feet, thereby surrendering to an agenda based on greed – his own sexual greed.

Equating me only with the flesh so that my role in life was to serve him! Today, I am no longer associated with his reign of terror;

for this cause, I give thanks knowing full well, it could have been worse.

To end this chapter, I'd like to reflect on a frightful situation which made me aware of his cruel and sadistic demeanour.

Where did this Level of Anger come from?

My younger sister was migrating to America and needed someone to take her to the airport. That morning, whilst I was on my way to school in Roger's car, I saw a parent that works for a taxi company. So, I asked Roger to try and catch up with him. The road was heavily congested, so Roger couldn't catch up with him and, unfortunately, he lost sight of him.

All I heard from him was "You have me driving down your man?" Without warning he turned the car into another direction. I didn't know where he was heading to but found myself on a lonely road which leads to a place called flat bridge. This is where two roads run between a deadly river. *Suddenly Roger took out a knife, held it to my throat; the kids started screaming saying, "Daddy, Daddy, please don't hurt Mummy." I was begging for my life. He then said to me, "You're lucky the children are in the car." That's when I knew this man was not to be taken lightly.*

My First Encounter of Faith

As time went by, I was given into solitude and contemplation to the effect that I was sick and tired of Roger's catalogue of lies, sexual manipulation, treachery, physical abuse, and violence. In effect, my mind went all the way back to the visiting Canadian Evangelist – Vanessa Anderson – who gently whispered, *"God has forgiven you."* I was feeling ashamed that having a child out of wedlock would cause the Church folks to reject me.

Through the confusing times I was experiencing, I made a

petition to God on the basis that if my wish was granted that was to deliver me from Roger's regime, then I would surrender to him.

I prayed for a breakthrough – that was the Saturday and by the Monday there was a knock at my door; it was one of my brothers outside claiming Dad wanted to speak to me.

Upon approaching him, not knowing what to expect, I was baffled to know what he wanted to say to me, with a bunch of keys in his hand. He said, "Your uncle called me and told me what you were going through.' Then he said, "Go live like somebody." Whatever he meant I came to believe there's a God and it doesn't matter how many times you have failed him, he never fails you. I was joyous that my prayer was answered. I was looking forward to starting a new life, me and my children.

Baffled as I was, it began to make sense the moment he mentioned my uncle from Canada, offering me the bunch of keys. This was my first testimony of faith and answered prayer.

Next day I couldn't wait to go and see this property which needed painting, this was my childhood home. For me at the time I didn't saw the transition as moving backward; going back to my old house where the turmoil was as a girl. All I wanted was peace, free from Roger and his nonsense.

When I went back there, I was happy to get an apartment. So, I started to scrub the wall, preparing it for painting. I went and bought a bucket of paint and started the work. Also, brought a stove, bed and dressing table. I got a fridge from my dad, again I was grateful for the help to begin a new life.

Again, he did something good for me. To be truthful I was grateful, even though the memory of how I was treated as a child came back to haunt me. Throughout the preparation to move, Roger never had a clue, I did it secretly.

CHAPTER 8

THE ESCAPE

For all the tricks in the book I didn't realise that this one would work, I decided to take the risk.

Mum was about to get a break to go work in Grand Cayman. This was how I would get away from Roger. I packed my suitcase with my children's clothes and mine and nothing else mattered.

I was willing to start life all over again. I hid the suitcase under the bed across from the room we occupied. The day of Mum's departure, I decided to accompany her to the airport then returned to let him know I was leaving for good. As I clutched my children close to me with suitcase in my hand, Roger looked startled, saying, "Where are you going?" His face looked flushed and numbed.

Can you believe he offered to take me to my flat? And I said yes. Frankly, I don't know why I listened to him, but I did What a fool was I. So, Roger escorted us to our new dwelling. However, where I moved to, was the same place within the community that I grew up as a child, so there's no way that was an escape to find peace, because he knew the address.

At the time it was a shift in address, but not safe. In Jamaica at the time when I was experiencing domestic violence, I don't think there was any accommodation such as a Refuge. There wasn't any safe place for women and children. We were left to the mercy of these men. Not sure what it is like today.

Dad intervened

This was what it took for Roger to be disciplined. I appreciated Dad's intervention. Fathers need to stand with their daughters so that they are not abused.

Leaving the abusive relationship with Roger, I thought the abuse would have been over but instead it got worse. Roger would come by uninvited. He would use the children as an excuse to keep an eye on me.

One day Roger decided to come by the house. As he drove on, he saw me talking to a neighbour. He started verbally abusing me by calling me names, this was so embarrassing.

As I wasn't living with him or having a relationship with him from where I lived, I was separated from this man, trying to rebuild my life and he took pleasure to disturb me at every opportunity he got.

One Sunday evening, I was at home in the apartment my dad gave me to live in. Roger came by, saying he was visiting the kids. I took the kids to him, and he sat with them in the car port. This is an addition to the house where visitors sat when they came to visit. I left him there with the kids and went back into my apartment to finish my dinner.

As I served the dinner to my younger brother, there comes Roger. He walked in and started to pass his remarks saying, "You refused to cook for me, but you are cooking for your brother?" I turned to him and said something, I guessed that upsets him. I can't remember what I said. The words couldn't come out of my mouth fully before Roger ran towards me in anger. I was heading towards my bathroom for refuge, and he followed me.

Suddenly, he grabbed me and started hitting me repeatedly. The punches were like two people in a boxing ring. All I knew that evening was that he pushed me down and next thing I ended up on an X-ray table at the Spanish Town Hospital.

When the doctor came to examine me, he asked, "What is wrong with you?" I responded, "My children's dad threw me on the floor during an altercation." He concluded, "He is a wicked man." That caused the middle bone in my bottom to shift. I still suffer from the fall. When I sit for a long time and try to stand up, I feel pain.

I didn't take a stand and discipline Roger for hurting me and that didn't let him give up on harassing me. Instead, it got even worse.

Roger increased his ways of how he would subject me to a life of misery. Every day Roger would watch my movements, either to or from work or going about other daily activities.

I became fed up but couldn't do anything about it because he was just too determined. My little brother would sometimes intervene but that didn't deter him from harassing me.

Roger didn't think he did me wrong and deserved to be punished. This is because no one had challenged him. So, he thought he had the right to constantly molest me.

This man was obsessed with me, he caused me nothing but unhappiness and misery. I was confused to why he was pursuing me when he was living with my sister. The moment I left the home, she moved in.

I knew this because one day I sent the children there and they came back and said, "Mum, Cecile lives with Daddy." I was hurt when I learnt that had happened. I never thought Roger would be so disrespectful. Also, I thought he would at least respect his parents. I guess when parents spoil their children that is what they will do to you. How could he eat his cake and have it at the same time?

CHAPTER 9

TRYING TO MOVE ON

Leaving Roger, I thought he would have moved on but instead he had his life on hold and surely put mine on hold too, but it wasn't for long.

About four years after leaving Roger, I felt the need to move on because remaining single might just give him the feeling that I was available for him.

No woman should be forced to have a relationship because she feared her ex won't leave her to live her life.

Attending a Church Barbeque

One Saturday evening, I was going to a Church Barbeque. As I turned out of my avenue, I realised a car stopped at my feet. The person asked, "Where are you going?" It was a private taxi driver. I was cautious of men. This was because of Roger's behaviour, and I wasn't ready to take any chances with just anyone. I was making sure the next man I met must be a person of faith and his priority must be his faith.

I said to the person, "Who are you?" Also, I said to him, "I don't accept a drive from strangers." He confirmed that he was working and that he had his own taxi business.

He insisted and said he would join me after he learnt I was going to a Church Barbeque, to which he did accompany me that evening.

During the journey we spoke, and he seemed polite. I was reluctant to have this man joining me at the function, but he insisted that his sisters were Christians, and he went to Church. Throughout the evening we talked, and he seemed nice.

So, after the barbeque we decided to be friends and that is how the friendship developed between us.

The Sunday morning, he came to pick up me and the children to take us to church. It was a good feeling to have my partner coming to church with me. Roger never followed me to church. He would take us to the church gate, drop us off and come to pick us up. That wasn't enough for me, I wanted someone who was willing to join me.

We were friends for a year. He seemed genuine, and never failed to come to church with us on a Sunday and acted with responsibility. He looked after the children like they were his; he had a daughter.

The children were happy until Roger found out; he wasn't happy and that was when the waters became troubled. He started to watch every move I made – when I left for work and when I was coming back home and who was taking me home.

Roger was jealous; how did I know? Because he passed a comment that "My man drives a better car than his." It is not the material things that I was paying attention to but, respect and integrity. Roger was a devious two-timer, double-minded man and a cheater. And certainly, he couldn't get anything because he didn't know what he wanted.

We tried not to let Roger's antics bother us, because he proved himself to be foolish. How can a man have his cake and eat it? I have a life to live, and I decided I wasn't going to let this man make me unhappy. Furthermore, he lived with my sister, so why couldn't I be happy?

After a year my we were engaged. His family were invited and my dad and one of my sisters were there too. It was an enjoyable day and I felt like this was a new beginning for me.

There is something I noticed with my dad's family. They only embrace people who are doing well, which is good but that is not all. Sometimes you can have men come into a woman's life as wolves in sheep's clothing. Especially when they realise you are single with children; they target you even more, thinking you are desperate.

For me all I need to know is that the person has ambition, is God-fearing, respectful, loving and kind. Also, willing to work. Even if you don't come with money but come with a plan and able to think.

One may ask if I would love my dad to intervene on a level that he sat with this guy and have a man-to-man talk? Yes, instead Dad just accepted the fact that he looked like someone who could look after me financially, which is important to every woman but what about being able to protect her. It's every man's duty to protect his family.

My point here is; there are other Jamaican parents who care about their children and protect them. I am not saying having my dad there didn't make me feel happy. I was trying to let Dad understand that he didn't protect me, his daughter, or my sisters from men who abuse women; this is because we all go through it.

Maybe he couldn't take a stand against such behaviour because he is guilty too, which is sad. I am not trying to embarrass my dad; every father needs to acknowledge that it is important to treat other men's daughters with respect that if someone is treating their daughter disrespectfully, they can honestly defend them.

That was part of his responsibility as a father. Ensuring his daughters are taken care of, especially knowing what I went through. I wished I had a dad who was more caring about his children's wellbeing.

I am not blaming my dad for everything that has gone wrong in my life. I must take responsibility for the choices I made. However, I strongly believe parents should be involved in decision-making. I must make it clear I am not bitter with my dad. I learn from my mistakes, and I am in a better place to make wiser decisions.

Back to Roger's antics. He knew I was engaged to be married because the kids would visit on weekends, and he would question them. Also, if he saw them in nice things, he asked them who bought them. To be honest, my husband used to buy nice things for me and the children.

Even his siblings were jealous of me. Talking about sisters, they were terrible women. He used to give me the best and they didn't like it. I remember he bought me a lace shower curtain and his sister came to the house and asked me to loan it to her, I said "No." From that day we never talked again.

After I was engaged, trying to live my life was challenging because Roger began to monitor my life. This man came across as if I did not have the right to a happy life. I guess that is what perpetrators do. They want to control and then they manipulate the individual.

One day my fiancé came for me at school. While we were on our way to my house, we saw Roger standing by the roadside with his friends. When he saw me, he didn't look happy? I knew he was planning something by the look on his face.

However, I didn't expect him to show up because my fiancé was with me. At least he could show some respect; but no, his plan was to ensure we were unhappy. I was on the veranda with my fiancé and the children outside playing when he turned up uninvited.

I am not trying to paint a picture like I was withholding the children from him. Roger knew it wasn't about the children; it was about monitoring me. Whenever he came by, he passed dirty remarks especially if he saw me talking to my neighbour and they are males. Those people I knew them from when I was a child.

Suddenly, I heard a raised voice outside and went to see what was happening. By the time I got to the door, there was Roger. As I reached towards the children to take them inside, he ran towards the grill and forced his way in. Was he there for the children? This behaviour confirmed his intention.

I couldn't stop him because he was already in. He was in a rage, suddenly he grabbed me and started throwing punches. I held onto him and was fighting back, but he overpowered me, because he was stronger.

I managed to get away from him and ran towards my brother's room; Roger saw me as I ran into the room and held on to the door. He pushed the door with force, and it fell off the hinges. That was a big fight between me, him and my fiancé who was defending me; that day I will never forget.

My dad was angry that Roger destroyed the door to the property and decided that he had gone too far, and he acted against him. I wondered if Dad was more concerned about what had happened to me or was it the door?

He thought Roger was mad to tear off the door and decided he must be disciplined. I saw the opportunity arise for me to get justice for all that he had done to me. It was a good thing that I was reporting the incidents as they arose; or what would I have as evidence. Dad got one of the best lawyers to represent my case, so we pressed charges.

It was after the incident I came to realise who was with or against me. The apartment where I had lived, my brother, his girlfriend and their children lived there too. His girlfriend was there the day when the incident took place but refused to give a statement to the police. I guess maybe she had feared for her life. I felt disappointed and hurt.

This was my first time having an experience in a Court room; I felt frightened, deserted and abandoned by my family. They knew how Roger had disadvantaged me and my sister and the time came for justice to be served but they walked away. I realised that this was going to be a long and lonely journey, but I was determined to get justice.

During the time going to court, things intensified between me and Roger and seemed difficult. I was feeling like my life was at stake. The situation looked daunting and life-threatening, but I wasn't shifting; I knew the reason why I was there. So, I persevered. The arresting officer saw that it was a difficult case because I didn't have any witnesses. However, I knew God would see me through.

At the time, my fiancé was my only support and was planning to migrate to America. This was because his mum filed for him. I used to tell myself that "It won't be long before I am left to fight this battle on my own." I was terrified of how I was going to get through this all by myself but when I look back, I realised God was with me.

The thought of testifying against the children's dad wasn't easy but I had to do it. Else he would think it was okay for him to continue abusing not only me but my sister too. She was just fifteen when he lured her into the lifestyle, she was part of.

During those difficult times, I thought my ex would adopt a neutral stance by staying away from me, since things were spiralling out of control, but he only made matters worse by perpetuating his brutal campaign of personal harassment and refused to give up!

CHAPTER 10

ROGER TOOK THE FIGHT TO THE SCHOOL COMPOUND

I remember whilst at work, Roger would take his protest to the school compound. I used to teach at a school that was situated on a church compound. So, that wasn't the ideal place for relationship issues, but I think he was trying to embarrass me, and he decided he would stop at nothing. Roger would turn up during lunch time. He would jump the gate and abduct our children from the classroom, throw them into his car, and drive off with them. I had to call the police every time he showed up at school.

His behaviour became frequent, and he was challenged by the police but continued. This went on for months, even when we were at court and the police gave him warnings not to come near me – but would Roger listen? I remember making a report one day and they said they were tired of his behaviour; "Do you want us to kill him?" they asked. All I wanted was for this man to see that his action was affecting the children, but he was too selfish to care.

He would find alternative ways to interrupt my life. One day whilst I was at school, my fiancé came for me. The timing was crucial. For some reason we decided not to go home but go shopping. Upon returning home, we were approached by my eldest brother, saying, "Girl, you're lucky today." I asked why. He said, "Roger and his friends came around here with guns to kill you."

I turned to him and said, "You witnessed this, yet you refused to stand with me to testify against him." At that moment, I was about to witness another side of my brother, my blood brother.

Suddenly, he ran off; no sooner did I realise he was coming towards me with a force, I noticed a machete in his hand. I knew it was me he was heading towards, so I ran.

My fiancé saw what was about to happen, and I ran off to take refuge in my bathroom. He pursued me through the room, trying to break off the bathroom door to come into the bathroom to kill me. I thought this was the end of me. I closed the door and used my body to push against it. I was frightened of his behaviour.

My fiancé shouted at him saying, "Man you are going to kill your sister?" At this stage he decided not to leave me there that night. So, I ended up in his mum's house that he occupied. I didn't want to move into his house before we got married, but the situation altered our plan.

Sudden U-Turn

We had planned that we wouldn't live together until we got married, but the situation changed our plan. He was living in a community that people are scared to visit and that is where I ended up that night, it is called Dela Vega City.

To be honest, you have good God-fearing people living there and it was a nice community too, the residents friendly and reached out to me and the children.

The houses were beautiful; seemed secure from my perspective. It was the safest for me at the time. The residents were tight knit in terms of looking out for each other. There was a lady who lived next door from me who I came to understand was a relative of my grandmother on my mother's side. They were very supportive of me and the children.

It wasn't long before my fiancé was preparing to travel, and I had to be strong for me and the children. I wasn't going to let Roger's bad behaviour break me.

It was hard for me as a woman, but I had to embrace hope and put on a brave front. I must say when my fiancé went to America, Roger never came into the community.

He stayed away but found alternative ways to intimidate me. For example, he would park on the highway across from the avenue where I lived. He did that, pretending that he wanted his children. He was using them as a scapegoat.

To be honest, there were times I felt unsafe, but I knew I had God protecting me. It wasn't long before the children wanted to see their dad and with prison hanging over his head, that wasn't an easy decision to make.

I wasn't planning to surrender to him; neither was I going to let the children sway my mind to our own hurt. This man had committed an offence and had to be disciplined.

I wasn't going to walk away from this battle; surely it wasn't an easy decision to make. The court case was strenuous and stressful, but I wasn't willing to give up my fight for justice. During the time when I was going to court, the arresting officer called me and said to me. "Why not give up, because it is going to be a long battle." I ignored him and pressed on.

The confusion of the children wanting to visit their dad was a mixed feeling – should I let them see him or not? However, I decided to let them visit and I used the home phone to communicate with them.

I tried to block the phone number to prevent him from getting through, but each time they were with him somehow, he managed to get hold of the number and started to harass me.

This time it was my sister too. They both would take turns on the phone to verbally abuse me and say unkind words to both me and my fiancé. The abuse became too much that we had to unplug the phone from the socket, to get a relief.

This caused my fiancé to be upset with me that I shouldn't give the number to the children. It may seem crazy, but I was only doing what I thought would make them happy and tried to be civilised to their father for their sake.

When he realised, he couldn't call the phone again, he would drive to the community and park along the roadside and watch our movements. If that didn't work, he would try other ways, such as going to the petrol station where my fiancé would park and create an argument.

CHAPTER 11

ALONE IN THE BATTLE

Facing something alone so daunting as a court case can be scary, but I embraced hope and carried on.

My fiancé left and spent six months away because of his job, and then came home and spent the remaining six months with me. I stayed away from Roger as much as possible. If he came for the children, I would take them out on the road and watch them run to him. He was a bit calmer once he didn't see my fiancé. It was when he came back from America that Roger lost control.

The battle at court was draining and some days I felt like giving up. Even the police officer tried to persuade me to give up. I sat in court on a particular day and surprisingly this officer walked over to me saying, "What are you doing here? You are a Christian, go home." I stopped and thought, is this the devil trying to make me feel guilty? I just ignored him and remained there.

Roger's mum was one of the main persons siding with him. She never told him when he was wrong. I think she never liked me from the beginning of meeting me. I believe violence and systematic abuse should not be tolerated in a humane society. However, it is a difficult battle to fight. Nevertheless, if we stand against it and confront the issue, we can reduce the level of rising cases.

Did she try to plant a seed in his mind to the contrary? He knew what he was doing was wrong. I must admit, his sisters remained neutral; they never treated me differently even when we were at court. Roger's prophecy of turning my sister's heart against me certainly came to pass, his behaviour was inhumane. What kind of a person targets people's family the way Roger did?

This man's intentions were evil; such notions ought not to be left unchallenged; my quest for justice had to be served. I was determined to show him that the walls of violence and abuse had to come down. Somewhere in his heart, he must be made to re-think.

I didn't give up and certainly wasn't afraid of all the threats that were levelled from his mum, my sister nor his friends. To be honest, I do not have a problem with his sisters. I am conscious of their continued respect throughout the whole of this dreadful saga. Whether we are Christians or not, domestic violence must not be tolerated. Not many have the guts to face their perpetrators, but for me in order to stop this man from killing me I had to do what was necessary.

My mission is to tell my story to empower and help women to gain courage, not to tolerate domestic violence or any forms of abuse. With this story, I hope many will gain courage to fight their way out of turmoil.

Isn't it time our men earn the respect due to them? Against a backlog of unreported and untold stories of violence and abuse against women, this whole subject becomes messy. Mine is just one tory, polka-dotted amidst a myriad albeit a catalogue of untold incidents!

The Day of Sentencing

This day was nerve-wracking, but God saw me through.

The day of sentencing was a happy day, especially for the children. A lot of women let these men talk them out of standing up for what is right. Nobody likes to be shamed or find themselves being arrested.

It was time for him to face the music and pay for his bad behaviour. Men must stop objectifying women and treat them like they are human. These men need to know that their wives or girlfriends are somebody's daughter. Also, if they have daughters – would they like another man to treat their daughter the way they are treating someone else's daughter?

Never mind being found guilty at the end of it all. In the face of the public and their opinion; it wasn't nice to see one of our country men being incarcerated because of domestic violence.

I am not here to gloat, or some may call it witch hunt; this wouldn't be in keeping with my mission. Somewhere an agency must be found to register a strong and clear message to the effect that violence will not be tolerated. This was a nerve-wracking experience for me.

He was sentenced for six months in prison. What did I feel for this man as he was led away? I pitied him to see what anger can do to a person. This is a man that I once loved, but did he love me with all he put me through? What was his definition of love?

What were the expressions written on his face? For a moment he looked bland, momentarily looking around before hanging his head in utter shame. I held on to my faith, knowing that God was on my side no matter what.

I remembered at one point during his incarceration, his lawyer pleaded for me to reconsider, so as for his sentence to be reduced. According to her, he wasn't coping well and he was losing weight.

A Poem

It was silence and then

You cared and that was a fact

But it's that time when you decided to snap

Reasons beyond my understanding

The rage, anger and then

It's either a fist, slap or the emotional isolation

How can I explain?

Tension beyond what words can express

All I wanted was for you to tell me what was happening

So we could work things out

I tried to reach out to you but you resist my love

My thoughts couldn't comprehend

Those brutal moments

The moments you had me thinking

But couldn't speak

My blood pressure raised

Because you left me no option

No voice or else

A slap, that's what silenced me

I was afraid of the repercussion

The isolation which tore my heart apart

How much longer can I bear

I am at breaking point

That point where I perceived

It's either now or never

I refused to remain silent

I must show some emotions

That I am being hurt

That moment when I think

Could this be the end, which ends in fatality?

Because of the inner rage that I see every time

I try to relate my inner feeling

The pain, the torment

It's easily seen in my eyes

Once told, there's a sadness that hides behind

Your true self

It's a mask, that I tried to hide behind

I said to myself one day

I will rise, I told myself

And speak, no more silence

I have a voice, I am human

I was created to be free

So, if it's the last time I speak

I decided to have a voice

Overcoming Difficult Situations and Survive

A voice which says, no more injustice

I'm me and refuse to be silenced by my circumstances.

CHAPTER 12

ABOUT TO BE THROWN IN THE DEEP

Some jobs just meant for some individuals and no one else can do it for you. Situations keep spiralling out of control, one thing after the other. My daughter was experiencing spiritual attacks and constant disruption if she was at church; it happened at school too.

Mentioning this is not to embarrass her but is to bring hope to someone who might be experiencing difficult times. I reckon why this was happening is, if readers remember when I spoke about going to a bush doctor. This is how this circumstance arose because a door was now open for these spirits to start affecting us.

It was about a few weeks into the situation and I was about to see the manifestation of these spirits in another form. There was a crusade at church one Sunday afternoon, whilst we were there enjoying the meeting.

My older daughter started to act uncontrollably. For example, foaming from her mouth, eyes began to change and sudden fainting spells.

Also, there was an unusual male voice coming from her, with her portraying an enormous strength if anyone tried to hold her. I remember a few of the ministers within the church, during a service tried to hold her, but she was too strong. She suddenly would burst into rage. It seemed unusual and was concerning that I was called into a meeting immediately after the service.

This Pastor was trained in deliverance ministry, so he wasn't afraid of ghosts or whatever it was at the time.

As he was talking to us, my daughter started talking like a man. This wasn't her usual voice but sounded like a monster. He spoke to her, talking to what was talking through her, saying "Who are you, and what is your purpose?" It said that "It was from hell, and its purpose was to kill her." That freaked me out, but I couldn't run because she needed me. I had to embrace hope knowing God was with me. It wasn't only her that I was having a problem with, it was also the younger one. She would complain about her tummy for weeks and I never knew what the problem was.

One day a voice said to me, "Go on a fast and lie on her tummy and pray for her." I did it and God healed her. With the other one who was severely affected with strange voices coming from her, that was more challenging. I just want people to know that evil exists, and it is real, and it can kill. It wasn't going to take her out though because I am a fighter and a winner through Jesus Christ.

The situation was become embarrassing. Thank God for those who stood with me with their prayers. This experience I will never forget and wouldn't want to experience it again in my life.

At the time I was beginning to think it was my fiancé's house that was the problem. I was going through a lot with Roger, his sisters, my sister and I don't exempt my mum – she was devious on the quiet. Who is to tell she didn't have a hand in this too?

I never forget my dad said to me that my mum did something to me, but he wouldn't say what, but later in life I would find out. I always question myself; why am I going through these battles? Something isn't right and I must find out. I was thinking all sorts to conclude what was causing the problems. I was even thinking also, if going to the bush doctor was what caused these spiritual problems. It may well be that was part of the problem too. God hates it when we turn to these people for help.

The situation intensified daily, causing confusion mentally and psychologically i.e. when my daughter started reacting, especially at school, my day would be interrupted by phone calls from her school saying I should come and collect her.

In all of what I was going through, where was Roger? He was the instigator to where he took me. Also, I volunteered to go, so that was my responsibility too. This went on for a long time until I started searching for answers. I had to start seeking God through fasting and prayer. I went on a three days' fasting and at the end of the fast God told me "That's your child and it was your job to deliver her."

Daily, I would engage in singing worship songs, then I realised she would become uncontrollable. She would run under the table and start to scream, and foam would come from her mouth. I cried many days when I saw her condition, I was worried but never gave up hope that she would get well one day. My faith was what kept me going until she eventually got better.

Throughout those difficult times, my fiancé was away, and I was examining my life and the situation I was in. I was thinking was this to do with his family, Roger, or whether the spiritual battle I was experiencing was coming from my fathers' house.

Was the Marriage a Trap?

I thought marrying my husband would change him; but I was wrong. If a person can't see where they are going wrong, it doesn't make sense if one tries to persuade them.

Mr Miller came across as if he was the type of man that would listen to his wife; but it's when we got married, I realised he was stubborn, angry, and bitter. At that stage I wished I could break away from the marriage but unfortunately, it was too late.

Also, Mr Miller knew how to manipulate me to marry him,

suggesting if I didn't then he would kill himself. It was long before I was convinced, and we set the day for the wedding. We got married on Valentine's Day 1998 and the marriage wasn't that great, but I decided to hold on, with the intention we would migrate one day and hopefully we would be happy.

I knew we had been through a lot and maybe what he experienced was affecting him that caused him to be difficult. I am not trying to justify his actions but trying to be reasonable. He is human, and people can get weary, especially if they aren't strong.

The reader might be wondering why I was running away from him but ended up marrying him. How I didn't sure he wasn't saying that to get me to where he wants me.

I talked about his kindness, but I came to understand that anyone can put on a front to get what they want; and after they get it they've gone back to square one.

His problem was that he didn't know how to resolve issues. I tried talking to him, encouraging him that silence wasn't the answer, but he ignored me sadly.

I tried telling him that there's no relationship that doesn't have disagreements, it is how you resolve them that matters. I remember he left for work one morning without telling me. This was because he was upset and decided not to talk.

Evening was far gone and there was not a sign of him. I waited for him during bedtime but not a sign of him, so I fell asleep. At about midnight, the phone rang. It was a hospital. The nurse said, "Are you Carrol?" I said, "Yes." She said, "I have your husband here."

I had forgotten that he was angry with me when he left for work and I asked what happened. He told me as he was turning a corner on a long winding country road, in St Elizabeth, Jamaica, his car went over the bridge.

I asked him how he got help; he said that someone saw him go over the bridge and called the police and fire brigade, according to him after waking from his unconscious state. Also, that it was a big stone that stopped the car from reaching the bottom until the rescue team came, they told him.

It is funny because that day whilst at home alone, I think the children were with their grandparents, I found myself praying for him. I remember Rod Parsley a TV Evangelist was on the television and I was enjoying the programme. God knew what was about to happen to him and sent angels to rescue him.

When he got home, I just encouraged him that it is unsafe to walk away from your spouse and refuse to talk especially if something is wrong.

Thank God he only had his neck in a cast for a week, it could have been worse. After that experience, one may think Mr Miller had changed his behaviour; not at all, he went back to his old behaviour.

He was as stubborn as an ox. What was he expecting when he got married? That he was going to live a life free of challenges? Keeping malice was part of him.

I was convinced something was wrong and only God knew what was happening to him because it didn't seem normal. No one can live with someone not talking to them. I cared for him because I remembered those times when he stood with me, it was important. So, I was willing to stand by him too, but he didn't give me a chance.

I felt powerless and couldn't help him; because he wouldn't allow himself to be helped, even his big sister and her husband came to talk with him, but he remained quiet. This sister I got along with; it's his dad's daughter.

Looking back, that was emotional abuse and it made me eventually became angry with him because I was hurting to see him like that, and it was too much to handle. Did something happen to him which caused him to treat me the way he did? The behaviour was abnormal.

An Encounter with a Spirit Being

People may be thinking, why I am having these experiences. A lot of people don't believe these things exist. I can see things before they've happened, it's a gift I was born with.

I remember one early morning about 4am, I woke up and decided to go and look through my bedroom window and there was a ghost sitting on the wall.

It freaked me out, but I wasn't afraid. So, I told it to move or else I would throw water on it. It looked at me and walked away and I never saw it again.

I am now thinking, was it his father? This was because he died soon after we met. Also, there was a time when I knew a spirit occupied my back room. I was determined that I wasn't going to live in a house with any ghost. So maybe that was it, and it left that night.

That encounter had brought back a memory of what I was experiencing that led me to go to a church service with a friend. She stopped by one evening and told me to go and see if the pastor could help me. So, I took her advice and went, she accompanied me.

When I got there the service was already in progress. I sat at the back and was observing what was going on. At the end of the preaching, he made an altar call to pray for those in need.

I wasn't going to step forward. This is because I felt embarrassed that he would find out what was happening to me and I just wasn't in for any surprise.

He said, "I am counting to ten for that person to come forward." I didn't pay any attention because I felt embarrassed for anyone to know what was happening to me, so I remained seated.

He was almost getting to the end of the count when I decided to get up. I slowly looked both sides of me and no one else got up.

As I walked towards him he said, "I never knew you would get up, because when you go back home it would be you and your duppies." He began to pray and break witchcraft curses from me and my children's lives.

That night was the night I never returned to my husband's mum's house. My other friend that was at the crusade said to me, "Don't go back there, come stay with me until you get somewhere to live."

At the time my husband was in Boston, and I told him what happened, and he agreed for me to move. It was funny but when he was away from that house, he would talk to me. I believe something, or someone, did something to this man. Why would he talk when he is abroad but not when he came home? It sounded and seemed spooky.

I never forget he told me his mum wanted to buy my wedding dress and he told her no; that made her unhappy. Why would she be unhappy? Was she planning something or was she genuine? I don't think she was because when she came, she was trying to discourage me from marrying him.

I was concerned about her behaviour as she was meeting me for the first time. So, why was she trying to put negativity in my mind about her son or was she jealous that he'd found someone? Some parents can be jealous of their children.

I do believe my mum isn't happy for me having a man around

me. It's the behaviour she displayed when I was having difficulties and went to her for support. Another way I have proven is when my sister got involved in me and Roger's relationship, and I went to her about it; she never seems bothered.

Not all in-laws are genuine, especially when they haven't got a man around them. My mum wasn't living with my dad and I could feel a negative energy when she used to come around the house when I used to live with Roger.

Regardless of my dad's behaviour, I still loved him and wonder if Mum felt I preferred him over her. To be honest, regardless of his weaknesses, he's the one that visited the children regularly.

Mum was aware that I had married but she never asked about my husband. Even though she was living in Grand Cayman, she must have heard. I don't think she liked to see me happy.

I have reservations about her because Dad told me she did something to me when I was a baby, but he wasn't going to say and that I would know one day. Also, one of my sisters always said to me that she treated all of us badly; but she knew I got it the worst. To be honest I knew she had something against me; but I can't put my finger on it.

Trying to keep these two in-laws at bay wasn't intentional but it was for the best. I am wondering was my husband's mother was the guilty party that caused him to get confused.

It wasn't long before he went back to Boston, and I thought it was better to end the marriage because I was suffering from the silent treatment which affected me psychologically; also, the harassment from his sisters.

His behaviour was drain on the relationship. I never forget his daughter's mum spoke to me about the reason she walked away from the relationship, that he didn't know how to deal with problems. Also, the malice of keeping the silent treatment.

I suggested he got help, but he wasn't co-operating. What could I do? You can take the horse to the water, but you can't force him to drink. Even his eldest sister and her husband got involved, trying to help him sort things, but he shut everyone out.

Moving to Another House

After few weeks at my friend's house, I decided to start looking for somewhere to live, which was a challenge. However, I managed to find somewhere in a lovely community – Ensom Acres, a beautiful community with lovely houses and it felt safe too. The rooms were big with an extra extension to the property consisting of an ensuite. Mr Miller was away, and I was enjoying somewhere new and had a rest from Roger and his madness.

My place of work was across from the avenue to where I lived. So, it wasn't any hassle to get to work. Also, the children's school was nearby, and they walked to and from school.

Mr Miller came to the new house, and he liked it because it was spacious and the community was peaceful; that was the best place I have ever lived. Again, lovely neighbours, they loved my children and the children seemed happy. Roger used to come by to look for the children. He was calmer because after he came from prison, he never disturbed my life like the way he used to do, he seemed resentful but never harassed me.

CHAPTER 13

THE LAST STAGE OF THE MARRIAGE

New revelation into the marriage. When Mr Miller came back from Boston, I realised something started to shift in my dream where the wedding ring was concerned. At nights when I went to bed, I would see the ring changing from silver to black on my finger. That was disturbing to me. I can see things before they happen, so therefore I am giving an account of what happened where the marriage is concerned. Also, the dream was recurring, but I couldn't understand it.

So, I approached a pastor about my dream to see if he could explain from the spiritual perspective what was going on. This person was occupying the master bedroom with the ensuite, with his wife.

He sat with me one night and began to explain what was happening to me. He revealed that the ring was loaded, meaning it was fixed by people who believed in witchcraft. I do not understand why some people will go to any lengths to get what they want.

During the marriage, I realised something was happening with it, and I noticed I wasn't feeling or having that love for him like when we had first met. Also, we were fighting regularly. It was because the marriage wasn't genuine which explains the mystery behind the misery. Anyway, the minister prayed for me and broke the curse.

It wasn't long before the relationship came to an end. This was one night when we had an argument and he left the house. I never saw him again; then I heard that he was abroad. Also, when I enquired about the filing, he claimed he put into Immigration for me and the children, but it was a lie.

CHAPTER 14

A NEW CHAPTER OF MY LIFE

After separation or divorce, an individual is left to reflect. Divorce and separation are likened to death. People find themselves going through a grieving process. I felt those emotions because I was broken, disappointed, felt shame and had lost something I had tried building.

I didn't marry to separate or divorce, I wanted it to last forever. I started to look back on my life and evaluate where I had gone wrong with my relationships. I think I wasn't giving myself enough time to think about counselling, which I didn't.

Talking about counselling, I wasn't aware of such support whilst in Jamaica. No one had mentioned that kind of help. I am surprised that the Church wasn't active, except for maybe a one-off which I had that experience, but I needed to have been referred for professional counselling.

My problems and demons that were affecting me came from my home environment. I came from a dysfunctional home where I wasn't taught love and affection or taught how to choose right. That is a parent's duty; to teach a child how to identify negative energy and stay away from it.

I know parents can teach their children, but that doesn't necessarily say that they must follow. I was left to fend for myself in every way. Remember, I was the older girl who had to take on certain responsibility because that is what happens in our family, the culture too.

Also, after the separation of me and my husband, I decided not to go back into another relationship but to take time to work on myself.

I spent time discovering what my hobbies could be and explored them. For example, I got enrolled onto a drapery designing course whereby I gained the skill to learn how to make drapes for people's homes. I would make curtains and bed linen with pillowcases to match.

Also, I learnt how to make little girls' knickers and boys' briefs, and dining table runners. Just about anything to keep me busy and productive. My skill had helped me to feed my children. The skill comes in handy after I had to leave my teaching job because of personal reasons.

There was a lady who I made a bed set for and whenever I go back home on holiday and go to look for her, she told me she still has it.

Dad Stepped in to Support Us

After the separation of my marriage, Dad came back on the scene and I was glad to have him even though he was awkward, still had his funny moods. However, that's what family is for, to help. There are bad times and good times and it's when we need family. I am grateful for him being there especially for the children.

During the time of recovery from the separation from my marriage, I called it, separation syndrome. I remember sickness struck where the children were concerned, and it was Dad who stood by us.

He would come to look for us frequently and he ended up sleeping at the hospital one night when one of his granddaughters was ill. I guess he loved those two girls and he also spoilt them. He would regularly bring cases of milk and fruit juices for them on a weekend.

Even though Dad used to come by regularly, I noticed he had a bit of resentment towards me. I think because he and Mum separated, it affected him, so he treated us differently.

There's an older sister who is not Mum's daughter, even though Mum raised her; I think Dad loved her more than my mother's children. My reason for saying this is everything he has, like assets, I came to understand is in her name.

When he left the family house after he and Mum separated, he never wanted us there anymore. I think something went wrong and there are some family secrets that someone is not sharing. How can a father not seem to love his children?

I know Dad wasn't the kind of father that loved his children to want to see them occupy his house and live there forever. However, I think he should have been more lenient, especially towards the younger one at the time when they needed a roof. Dad refused to be compassionate and told them to leave.

One day I was reflecting why Dad was cross with me; I realised it was because he wanted my youngest brother out of the house and I challenged him that he was too rough and should be more loving to his children. During those days my younger brother was struggling, and it wasn't that he was being disrespectful towards Dad. It was Dad's regime, that we should leave at seventeen.

At that time, my brother was still a teenager about 18, and most of us were already out of the house, so there was enough room for him. I said to Dad that was the very reason why all of us struggled and that if he couldn't treat my brother better, I didn't want anything from him for my kids. That night he went into a rage and from that day he never showed me kindness again. I loved my brothers and sisters and didn't want to see my younger brother struggle.

As a child, I never felt free to express my feelings, fears and disappointments with Dad and that made me suppress my hurt, and later I realised I was beginning to become an angry person.

I found out I couldn't deal with issues calmly and would find myself shouting. That was hard for me, and many people even my children couldn't understand that I was a wounded person.

I never felt cared for as a child and Roger violated that again. He took disadvantage when he knew the upbringing I had. What a heartless man he was.

I cared for everyone else, but no one stopped to care for me. However, I therefore love to help people now. I am an empathetic person; I think it's because of what had happened to me.

After my husband left, Dad supported me with the kids in terms of taking cases of milk and juice for them. When the struggles started, sometimes he would tell me to bring the children over to his house. Dad was weird, I think he wasn't shown love as a child; therefore he couldn't give what he didn't get.

The kids loved him, especially the younger one. She used to go to the lemon tree, pick the lemon and take a glass, put sugar in it and add water and ask Dad to cut the lemon and make him lemonade. She use to drop the lemon into the glass of drink and said, "Here Grandad, drink juice." I guessed he loved both children. The other one had her moments with him too. Also, the younger one would follow him everywhere he went.

If he said he couldn't take her, especially if he was going to work, she would hide his shoes and when he asked for them, she would say, "You not getting them Grandad unless you take me with you." She was a little madam.

My dad had multiple personalities; in terms of he would be doing yet good to me, yet still doing me bad. There are many things

I haven't mentioned because it sounds awful and need not be repeated.

One might say, but her dad did come back into her life and did well. My grandparents would say, "if not everything good to eat, good to talk". I think I've said a lot for anyone to get a full picture of the situation.

CHAPTER 15

LIFE FROM A DIFFERENT ANGLE

Back at square one, but I didn't give up, I fought my way to victory. Never give up when the going gets tough.

It wasn't long before I lost my job and things became challenging for me. I was twenty-eight years old, and my life was just going downhill.

I decided to step out of my comfort zone and explore the impossibilities e.g. to throw myself into the deep. Firstly, I joined the choir at my local church. Joined the drama group and acted as the main character in different plays; this made me feel confident. Suddenly I started to feel lighter, becoming braver and I found my freedom to fly.

My faith reached another dimension. I recall the year early (1999); I was unemployed; and went to the Immigration Department, Spanish Town, Jamaica, West Indies, to apply for a passport.

As I was in the queue waiting to be attended to, I realized that there wasn't anyone there. So, I stepped to the front of the queue and rang the bell, and an Immigration Officer came and asked me if he could help.

I said to him, "Why is the queue getting longer and no one comes to attend to us?" The officer said to me, "There isn't anyone permanent to work in that position because the person who works there is on holiday." I bravely said to him, "Can I get the position?"

He looked at me with curiosity and asked why I was interested and said, "If you are serious, go to the Head Office Monday morning and speak to the Chief Immigration Officer there." I did what was suggested.

The following Monday morning I turned up and asked for the Chief Immigration Officer; a woman stepped forward asking if she could help me. I said to her, "I was at the Spanish Town Police Station Immigration Department on Friday, waiting for someone to attend to me regarding the renewal of my passport, but there wasn't anyone there."

So, I made an enquiry about the position and was told there was a vacancy; and that's why I was there to have a talk with her. She told me there were a few other applicants before me who were interested in the job, but she would give it to me because I was brave.

My Experience at Passport and Immigration

My first day at Passport and Immigration. It was a new experience. Working in a new environment occupying the position as a Civil Servant was fascinating and interesting.

I worked in the department where passports were being produced. My job was to cut the passport photos to fit into the passport and enter personal information. Also, to place them into the right compartment to send to different departments before they are dispatched for Royal Mail to be delivered to applicants.

Working in that department was tricky because one had to ensure the photos are cut to the size to fit the section they will be placed, without error. Also, we had to ensure that the correct spelling of applicant's information was written on the application.

Any error can be tedious and time-consuming to correct. So, the job called for concentration. I worked there for few months as a

Clerical Officer. I didn't work there for long because I was planning to migrate to America to pursue a degree in Nursing.

However, my plans got altered and I changed direction and decided to come to the United Kingdom after my marriage failed.

CHAPTER 16

CHANGE OF DESTINATION

I felt like it was time to move on. If you find yourself at a place and things seem not to be working, that means it's time to shift location. However, sometimes it might be a phase you are going through and you just need to turn your attention to different possibilities. For example, it might be the loss of a job. It might just be that the need to think about starting a business is the best option. Not everyone likes taking chances, but employers take a chance and that is why they can provide work for people. Most of the time it's fear that keeps a person from plunging into the deep.

After leaving Passport and Immigration, it was time to draw upon the skills I learnt, and which became useful; drapery and designing. I bought two industrial machines and two over-lockers and got another person to work with me. I started to make draperies and bedroom accessories.

My faith is something I rely on to keep me connected to God for direction on what to do. It wasn't whilst someone was praying for me, but I heard him saying, "Get your passport ready you are going to travel." I was baffled – what was he saying or what did he mean?

I felt optimistic about travelling but, "where to," I asked myself. I remembered one day while I was walking from church one Sunday afternoon, a small voice said to me, "Go on a twenty-one days' fast." I didn't understand why I should go on a fast, so I ignored this and carried on with my everyday tasks.

It wasn't long before things started to make sense. One Saturday morning I went to a women's conference and saw a woman I was familiar with. She ran up to me and said, "Girl, I'm going to England, and I am not leaving you." That was when I started putting the pieces of the puzzle together, the prayer, and to go on a twenty-one days' fast. So, I went home and started packing. I called my landlord and told her I was going to migrate; she thought I wasn't serious until she realised – I sold my furniture went to my friend and stayed for the duration of the fast.

I began my spiritual journey, and it wasn't long before everything started to fall into place. For example, my uncle from Canada called one day and I told him my plan to go to England, but I didn't know anyone. He paused and said, "We have a cousin living there," and that he would put me in contact with her; that's my dad's cousin. I got $16,000 from selling the furniture then the remaining $32,000 dollars was later given to me by other family members. That was how my plane ticket was paid for; also, I was put into contact with another cousin to tell her that I was going to the UK.

I beginning to think how I was going to make my escape without Roger knowing. So, I called him and asked him to have the kids for the day to take them out for a treat. My heart was racing, I had mixed feelings about separation from the children. It was all sorts going through my mind but regardless I kept focus.

The Day of Departure

That night leaving; I had mixed feelings of hope, and despair. This was because I was leaving the children behind. I had to move like a detective with calm and with skilfulness. Not even my neighbour whom I was talking to that day knew I was migrating. As a matter of fact, I gave up the house I was living in and stayed with a friend.

Leaving for the airport that night, the feeling of sadness overwhelmed me. I never thought I would have to leave my children behind because of Roger. I was feeling worried that he would try to monitor my movements and try to stop me if he knew, but I managed to get to the airport without him having a clue.

It was one of my friends who accompanied me to the airport with the children that night. Looking back; I don't think it was a good idea having them come to see me off. The reason is; I believed it had caused stress on them that night.

Also; I asked the girls not to say anything to their dad when they went back home; but wait until I cleared Immigration and reached my destination, and then I would call to let them know I arrived safely.

CHAPTER 17

ADAPTING TO LIFE IN A DIFFERENT COUNTRY

I arrived in the UK late at night; the year was 2000 and everything seem different. I remembered coming through the airport and people was rushing everywhere. It was a feeling of happiness that at last I was away from Roger. The feeling felt great, but a feeling of loneliness swept over me; I missed my children.

Looking around me, I could see people from all walks of life which makes it interesting. I sat on a chair for a long time waiting to be seen by the Immigration officer. When she did find the time to attend to me; she said, "I am so sorry to have kept you waiting."

Then she said, "Follow me." She took me to a room where she asked me to put my suitcase on top of a table; a gentleman was there, and he put my suitcase on the table for me. I have never seen such politeness before, she was lovely and welcoming. Not to mention when she opened the suitcase and found yellow yam packed neatly that my cousin told me you can't find in the UK. Also, Jamaican juicy beef patties and anything else that I could find to pack in terms of food was in the suitcase. Looking back my cousin was cruel you know; she told me there's no yam in the UK. Maybe if a donkey could get into the suitcase, she would have told me to pack him too – smile!

I was taken to a room whereby my suitcase was checked and then I was taken back to sit down in the waiting area.

Later, I was called and taken through to a room to be asked some questions which some had to do with my cousin who came to receive me and how often she and her family visited us in Jamaica. I knew the answers because she would visit regularly, and she stayed with her mum, and we would visit them with Dad. Then I was asked to go back outside and sit down.

It was a long wait, and I was wondering how long before the wait came to an end. I felt optimistic, enthusiastic, mixed with sadness because the children weren't with me. I started missing them. As I walked through the long corridor leading to Immigration all sorts of things were going through my mind. For example, what questions would they ask, and suppose I was asked a question I didn't know the answer.

Leaving my country of birth, the way I did, was very sad and remorseful. As I approached Immigration, all I could see was men and women smartly dressed and passengers running around. I felt frightened yet brave, scared yet courageous. I was put to sit in an area whilst other passengers from where I'm from were being looked after, and ethnicity too.

It was a long wait before I was called to be questioned. The Immigration Officer was very kind, co-operative and welcoming. The process took a long time which I understood.

A question was asked about one of my cousin's children which was vital for me to know. So, when I gave the answer, the Immigration Officer said to me, "Wait there, let me check with your cousin and come back to you." That question let me through that night, and we were on our way to her house.

Her husband and the children were at home waiting to see me. They were happy and we chatted that night and shared a lot about my journey to the UK. Shortly after we arrived and settled, my cousin asked, "Are you going to call the children to tell them you landed safely?" That moment was a feeling of happiness and mixed with sadness because I wish we had all got away at the same time. I dialled the number; it was in the morning in Jamaica, and it was Roger who answered the phone. Like an angry child, he huffed and puffed; and if he could catch me, he would blow me away like the big bad wolf! He angrily handed the phone to the children and so as they were glad to hear my voice, I too was happy.

CHAPTER 18

MY COUSIN'S HOUSE

The following morning my cousin woke me up to tell me I needed to go to work with her. She owned a hair-dressing business. I went, even though I was jet-lagged because I wanted to see as much of the UK as possible, meaning where she was. She travelled by bus so I could see places, communities which were beautiful.

I accompanied her to the nursery where her daughter went. The following morning was the same routine, to go to her hair-dressing parlour to sweep up after her and I could be sure to get a McDonald's meal at lunch time.

Something strange came across my mind one night; it was like someone saying to me to put my passport into my bosom. I don't know why that crossed my mind, but I followed the thought. I went to bed that night and upon waking I realize my suitcase had been ransacked.

I asked her if she knew who went into my suitcase, she said that it was her. I asked, "What for?" She said, "I want to send you back home." I was so disappointed in her behaviour, how can a relative be so cruel, what had I done to her? I asked her, "Was it you who bought my plane ticket?" I was grateful for her assistance to welcome me into the UK; but that didn't give her the right to want to manipulate me and suggest she wanted to send me home – tell me about family!

One morning I realized my cousin's mood swings. She began to mumble that when she goes on holiday, she takes her own money to feed herself, she doesn't depend on anyone. I didn't leave with any money because I didn't have any. I was facing a life and death situation and had to take chances. All I left Jamaica with, was saving grace and my suitcase.

Week three; she started to behave like a different person, as if we weren't relatives. I came to understand, as I get to understand how people behave, that once you come to the UK you better not stay at relatives' house for more than a few days, or else they will show you a cold side.

That is the way they tell you; you've outstayed your welcome. So, it wasn't long before I was feeling depressed and lonely. It was a good thing I knew where to find my other cousin. The one I mentioned earlier; or else I would be doomed. I never forget she told me she and my father had a conversation to the effect; I guess whatever it was it had a negative affect on her that caused her to change suddenly towards me.

Her Plan Didn't Work

She pretended that she was with me all along when she came to the airport, but she was an enemy in disguise.

What happened to my nice cousin? She had changed into a different person. What was that for I don't know; she is a woman too and should look after me, also a relative. She may not go through what I have been through; and certainly not because I have experienced difficult situations doesn't give her the right to treat me less. What has this world come to? People are so mean. However, not everyone is like that. I admire the Asians, they are so united – why can't some of us adapt like other people and how they express love.

It wasn't long before she came up with a plan to finally get rid of me. One morning she got ready for work, she turned off the phone, and left me indoors with the door open; she didn't lock it with the key. That meant I couldn't go out because the door would close on me because it was one of those locks that if you go out it locks you out.

I managed to find a telephone directory and I used it to block the door and quickly ran to the phone box. I had one 20p and that was how I got in touch with my cousin, that is my first cousin, my dad's sister's child.

I only could be brief and tell her to call me because it was urgent. I stood at the phone box and waited for the return call and then told her what was going on with my cousin. She told me she was going to get help for me.

She knew where I was living because she used to visit that cousin and she didn't speak well about her. I went home and no sooner did a car pull up at the gate and there were my cousin and another relative, my dad's uncle.

I never met him before. They knew how difficult she could be and decided that I must leave. I couldn't leave the house unprotected, so I waited until she got home.

I learn to value what people do for me, even if they are horrible to me. Also; I do believe God sends people our pathway to help us and it doesn't matter if they help us fully, he will send someone else to pick up from where that person left off and continue the journey.

So, never feel deflated when someone comes, tell you they will help, begin, and walk away. They have done their path, thank them and move on or be grateful that God can send the other person that you would need to take you to your destination.

As soon as she got home, I told her I was leaving. Before I could finish uttering the word "leaving", she went upstairs and put my suitcase in the hallway and said, "Go." She didn't realize I had found my other cousin because when I was coming to the UK I was in communication with that cousin and told her where I was going to stay. Also, she had me call her as soon as I arrived and that was how I held on to the number.

When she saw my great uncle and my cousin pull up at her gate, she said, "I thought you said you didn't know any family." See, I use wisdom; I always have a backup plan that when the devil strikes, I am covered. God calls fool but he made us wise if we listen to that small still voice.

CHAPTER 19

MY UNCLE'S COUSIN'S HOUSE

Moving from one place to the other because someone chooses to oppress another individual isn't easy but, for my sanity, I was glad when I got the opportunity to move on. Thanks to her, else I wouldn't be where I am today.

After I left my cousin, my great-uncle called another relative of his, asking him to rent me a room. It was nice to meet that great-uncle because he took me to meet other relatives.

Going there to live was good for me because I had peace of mind and began to focus a little more on enjoying the UK. That relative along with my great-uncle did feed me, until I started to put weight on. I was happy but still thinking of the children. So, it was a mixed feeling which was expected because I never separated from them. I started attending church with my great-uncle who used to come on a Sunday morning and pick me up from Norbury and take me to Croydon to church.

The church folks loved me because I use to sing, and they enjoyed my singing. Oh, I felt a freshness of glory, it's like I started living again. The thing that I loved to do was happening, which is to sing. I met some good people, both male and female. My uncle was paying the rent for me to live at his relative's, but soon it became a strain and sadly I had to leave and go to live with him and his wife who had dementia.

CHAPTER 20

MOVING TO A NEW HOUSE

House moving has never been easy, especially when you're from a different country. However, I managed to survive.

This time I had to move into my great-uncle's two-bedroom house, where he lived with his wife who had dementia. This was the first time I learnt about the illness. She was a clean lady, lovely to speak to, but she kept her distance. They were separated but lived in the same house.

I was now occupying the settee as my bed. I found myself getting to know different places, meeting people from all walks of life, also other relatives. I never knew my family was that large. I always feel at home or feel a vibe of Jamaica when I see someone, another black person, from back home.

For me, it was a culture shock, because seeing people from diverse communities and walks of life made it interesting. That diversity alone made me realize I was in a different country.

People from different countries and their languages sounded so different and interesting. The different accents blended sounded strange, perhaps stranger than the standard English with the mixed cultures.

I became accustomed to the different accents, whether it was in the marketplace where people were buying fruits and vegetables or on a bus, but they all sounded lovely. Not to mention the currency which seemed so different from what I used to; it wasn't easy to adapt to the new way of life; to understand it at the time.

As for the people, it struck me how diverse they were. I felt hopeless at recognizing who was Scottish, Irish, Welsh – never mind those from far-flung regions within Europe, i.e., Polish, French, Swedes, Germans, Italians and so forth. Amazed by the thought of some Asians or Africans having a background of anything up to four or five languages made me feel like working harder to appreciate the common bond of cultural differences. How beautiful they all looked in national costumes, especially during carnivals, not forgetting the whole variety of foods apart from the likes of fish and chips. There is something special with fish and chips here in the UK, it's nice.

I was beginning to feel safe now my relative was putting me in touch with family relations I hadn't even heard of. Better still, taking me to college to enroll onto a basic computer course along with Maths and English. As my sponsor, my great-uncle, was providing enough motivation for me to complete the City & Guilds Maths and English also Computer Programming, I managed to obtain a certificate. After careful reflection on my achievement at my first college, I realized I wasn't satisfied in terms of career choice.

So, I got enrolled at another college to pursue the Access to Teaching Course. At this stage I realized that I was struggling with tense, grammar and sentence structure.

So, I was advised by my personal tutor at college to re-enrol on the Access to Teaching at foundation level which would get me up to the level to manage the Access Course. I took his advice, and after one year I obtained the pre-Access Certificate which allowed me to enrol onto the Access to Teaching course; which I completed and obtained my certificate. At this stage my determination had paid off and I was now feeling overjoyed.

Thanks to the Home Office for extending my visa application which allowed for a further year extension which was great news.

Whilst waiting for my second extension, one morning whilst at home I realized there was a knock at the door. It was the postman; he said, "Can you sign for this please." I signed, took the envelope and opened it, realizing it was for me, my passport and a covering letter from the Home Office. I said, "Uncle, my passport came." He didn't seem too pleased as he uttered *"You turn somebody now!"* What did he mean? It wasn't long before I realized his attitude changed towards me.

Relationship Turns Sour

Over a period, believe it or not my uncle changed, and I was about to realize he wasn't looking at me as a niece anymore but someone he was interested in; relationship-wise. I was disappointed because I loved my great-uncle and never expected him to be like that. Also, I have never dated one of my relatives before and certainly I wouldn't. Also, because I wasn't that way inclined, I was now experiencing rejection from him. Can one believe what was happening to me? It left me feeling confused and hurt. What is happening to me, I was beginning to think?

I had plans on saving enough money to purchase my children's air tickets to come and join me. *"This is not a good idea,"* his remarks were *"for a start, you haven't got any place to accommodate them."* I thought he would support me sending for them.

All I required from him was a roof over my head. As tension rose between us, he started keeping a close eye to see if any guys from church were talking to me. For instance, he became overly protective. It made me feel pressured and confused.

One day, by coincidence while I was out and about, I met a friend from back home who had nowhere to live. So, I took her to my uncle, asking him if she could stay with us with until she found somewhere.

Thankfully, he agreed. This was a good way of diverting him

from bothering me. I remember mentioning it to my dad and he said I was lying because his uncle was respectable and wouldn't do something like that. I realized my dad was stuck in his ways. Maybe he hadn't been watching the news or he is just stuck in his own way. It wasn't long before I decided I was going to move out; this was after my sister, my dad's big daughter, came to join me in the UK.

I was the one who invited her and sadly she came and decided to treat me like a stranger. Can you believe, I invited her to come, went to the airport to pick her up, asked Uncle if she could stay with us – he said yes, and she turned around and betrayed me?

This was after one day when I was going upstairs; one of my cousins, the same one who came to pick me up after my cousin threw me out, was there at the house and I overheard her saying to my sister. "Don't come here to turn into a slave to look after Carrol's children." I don't know how she knew I was planning to bring the children to the UK. She certainly was a little piece of work whenever I was not in college and volunteering in a nursing home. This was with the intention of getting a job after my time volunteering.

At the time I managed to find myself work in a launderette where I worked when I was not at college. After three weeks' volunteering, I was offered a job whereby I worked for three years in a nursing home. That was where my passion came from to look after the sick and elderly. I worked in all aspects of care – Dementia sufferers, people with Parkinson's disease, Mental Health, Learning Difficulties, Palliative care, Support work – I have done them all.

I was unable to stay any longer at my uncle's because I couldn't cope with the stress on every side. So, I moved out and found accommodation in a place called Peckham where I rented a two-bedroom flat with a friend of mine from work; she was a lovely lady, she could be my mother she was old enough. We had a good time living at that flat. One night coming from work I was standing at a bus stop and met this person call Val and we talked until we became friends. He used to visit me at the flat where I lived whilst studying and working.

However, there was an issue at the flat whereby every time we went to work strangers would be in our kitchen eating our food, so the place wasn't safe and I was glad for the phone call of another relative who invited me to come to live at his mother's house – she had died leaving the house for him and his brothers and sister.

CHAPTER 21

AT LAST AN OPEN DOOR

An opportunity arises for me to find some where to live as well as not paying rent but utility bills. Also meeting a man call Val, the first relationship since I migrated.

Having met this guy called Val, we kept in touch and spoke regularly. One day whilst at home, the phone rang, I thought it was Val; but it was a cousin I hadn't met.

"I am only a phone call away," said a warm, comforting telephone voice.

"Who are you?"

"I am your cousin from your dad's side."

"Where did you get my number from?"

"Your sister gave it to me," said the person, a polite male voice. "I know it's not the best news you want to hear, but my mother has died leaving a five-bedroomed house; as it stands, one of my brothers is living there – would you like to live there too?"

I said yes.

As the conversation progressed, I realized it was an open door, hence a solution to the discomfort I was experiencing where I was living. I could hardly believe that a door was opening for me. I was asked only to pay bills which was a good gesture, for me to save for the preparation to get the children here to join me.

Val was becoming more than just an ordinary friend. He told me he lived as a single man in a one-bedroomed flat –insisting he wanted me to visit and see from the contents of his wardrobe, that there was no woman in his life – in the same breath offering to help me get settled in my new place.

No sooner than moving in, I noticed something rather unusual about my wonderful cousin. From what he told me, he paid regular visits to his mum's grave. i.e. every Sunday morning at a specific time. To be honest, I found this too weird – going to a graveyard to lay flowers in memory of loved ones, is unacceptable for me. This was new to me and my culture. Frankly, I couldn't understand why he needed to visit every Sunday morning. However, that was something he took pride in doing.

Running Checks on Val

After leaving Jamaica, after the breakdown of my marriage, I wasn't prepared to take any chances without doing a thorough check on anyone who wanted to form a relationship with me.

Another concern I had regarding; Val what did he do for a living? According to him, he was a Postgraduate within the legal profession so, he had experience with Immigration matters. That was important for me as an immigrant because; I needed to know what to do whenever my visa was coming to an end. However, he didn't practise within that field. Instead, he worked at a university as an administrator, but his friend practised within that capacity.

I really wanted to check this man out to find out what he said was true. Doubting his sincerity would be difficult especially that he dressed smartly, was well-spoken, well-mannered, sporting an attaché briefcase. He always invited me to restaurants, insisting on paying the bill. Still, there were reservations in my mind; for instance, it might be useful to ask neighbours living within his own location if they knew anything about him.

Soon after he introduced me to a female cousin of his; living next to his block of flats; telling me he was the one who brought her into the country. On a one-to-one, I approached her in a friendly manner just to find out if she could tell me anything about him that she would share in confidence, but she seemed tight-lipped; all she'd say was *"He was the one who helped me to come to the country."* "Yes; but what is he like?" All she was trying to say basically, is that he was a good person, trying to help others, end of story.

It wasn't long again before I met another cousin of his; this one was a male. I tried to get information out of him to what sort of person Val was; but again, he was too tight-lipped, because he was invited to the UK too, by Val.

He didn't have much to say other than Val was a good person. Seemed like everybody has been rehearsing the same song and got it right. Anyway, I went with the idea "He is a good person". I am not disputing that he didn't do good for me too, it's the lies that caused the mistrust between us, also he didn't protect me and my children.

CHAPTER 22

VAL DID A GOOD DEED

In every bad person, there is good. I am not saying Val didn't love me. Maybe he was torn between having multiple relationships and became confused or was that just his lifestyle. If he was honest to me, I'd rather be good friends with him other than to create complications for myself and the child we caused to come into this world.

As our relationship plunged to deeper levels, we became intimate. There were those times when I felt weak to the point of abandoning all my reservations; torn between the love of my daughters in Jamaica, and a man venturing on the threshold of my life at times was too much. Like the pages of an open book, Val read my mind day after day and night after night until one day he stopped me in my tracks:

"I will grant you the desire of your heart; don't worry about a thing; your children will be here sooner than you think." *"What?"* (Turning my head slowly.) The next day whilst escorting me into town for a meal, he diverted to the nearest travel agent and therewith paid their fare to come to join me on a holiday visit. So, I was drawn by his generosity and hoping this man didn't deceive me.

Arrival of Lucy and Sandy (not their real names)

With the flight booked and date all set, there was only one week left for my two daughters to arrive for their holiday, and it was a moment I looked forward to. By way of preparation, I had already furnished the room my cousin gave me to welcome them. The year was June 2001; the girls arrived, and it was a dream come true, thanks to Val. This was revealed to me even before it happened in a dream, but I never shared that with Val, I kept it to myself until it became reality.

The Day the Children Arrived

Preparing the morning to go to the airport was nerve-wracking for me. I had mixed feelings whether there would be a smooth transition for them, or a delay would take place.

However, whilst waiting for the children outside the arrivals area of the airport, an alarm went off while we were both seated. Everyone was instructed to vacate the area until the place had been thoroughly checked.

This was registering a different message, i.e., that God is about to manifest through the storm. So, His Purpose could be fulfilled. Crowds left and re-assembled with anticipation as we all encroached on the barrier.

From a considerably long way, all I could see was Lucy running towards my direction with her Pullman case behind shouting "Mummy, Mummy!!!"

Fighting back the tears, by now my tears were synonymous to giving birth to my offspring all over again. As Sandy was running as well then, I said to myself this is not a dream it's real. Then she shouted, "Mummy!!" and with a glint of promise written all over their faces, I ran and hugged them.

It was a happy feeling that day. We needed time to catch up. Quiet time to bury our faces as we acknowledged a successful rescue-mission from out of a quagmire of loneliness.

Oh what a reconciliation! What beauty enthroned in such love!

Love is like a bond that can never ever be broken Here we are again; by way of a human instrument chosen for this successful operation, I must accord special thanks to Val who stood with me through those lonely days and months, so much so, he was inspired to finance the air fare of my two daughters. For what turned out to be the happiest day of my life! Thanks Val.

CHAPTER 23

SUDDENLY REALIZED I WAS PREGNANT

Certainly, I wasn't planning for things to go the way it went but it was a blessing in disguise. Also, I have no regret having my daughter, she is a very warm and loving child.

As the relationship between Val and I grew, it dawned on me that we were headed in the direction of raising a family. Finding out I was pregnant, I thought Val would decide for us to settle as family.

With no word from him, this was leading nowhere within the first week of my children's arrival, the atmosphere was jubilant with celebration: now the whole thing was turning into shock because I wanted education – not another child!

However, I didn't let this divert me from my goal which was to pursue education. Although this child was not planned, I thought she might well be a blessing in disguise.

I had to work part-time whilst studying and looking after the other two children. After my daughter was born and after my discharge from hospital, I suddenly realized I started to experience a rush of anger compounded with increasing anxiety. I didn't understand what was happening to me. It was confusing and there wasn't anyone to talk to about these feelings. Also, would anyone understand what I was experiencing?

This went on for months and I wasn't diagnosed with depression that I could understand the complexity of the problem I was experiencing. It was long after I started to understand what was happening to me. I never had my health visitor asking me how I was feeling after the birth of my baby so I could explain the feelings to possibly have some conclusion to what may cause the sadness and rage I was experiencing. I started to learn about these mood swings by watching TV.

I had no idea I was suffering from Post Natal Depression. With mood swings leading further into aggression, I started shouting uncontrollably at my two daughters, at times even chasing them through the house. I didn't understand what was happening to me.

Val was in shock as to why I was behaving so weirdly. I am not sure he understood what was happening to me too. The truth is, I was in shock of another child as a single mum, and I was frightened as to how I was going to look after the three children on my own.

Also, my blood pressure was high; with guilt and mixed feelings my mood was at its lowest ebb. Also, the thought of going back to work after a six-week break was a stress. Not to mention going back to college three times a week to fulfil my Visa requirements, that was too much. God knows how I was going to cope with all the drama that had been going on in my life. However, I had to embrace hope and get on with the everyday tasks.

CHAPTER 24

DRIVEN FROM THE HOUSE WHERE I WAS LIVING – BY A GHOST

This is not easy for anyone to comes to term with what I'm about to share. Ghost, evil spirit, call it what you like but they are real.

Just before I moved out, I had a dream one night as I slept: A woman came to me in my dream and said, "You better come out of my house!" Not many days later, I went for an afternoon nap and saw myself struggling because someone was attacking me; I was shouting "help! help!! help!!!"

My cousin was living at the house at the time, and in the dream, I saw that he looked at me and walked away; when I woke up it bothered me. One morning not long after the dream, his son came to the door of the bedroom and knocked forcefully saying, "You better come out of my grandmother's house." This when the dream made sense to me.

Under these circumstances I didn't want my kids to become frightened and sick, so I decided to leave. It was at that point that I called a Church Sister who was working at a Women's Refuge. She decided it would be best if I moved in with my children the same day.

Even though I was not exposed to any physical danger, the fact is, I was psychologically and emotionally traumatized. Now that I needed Val more than ever, he just was not there for me. Not long after moving in the Refuge, we were told we had to leave because of Immigration status. I must admit living there was a good memory for us; they looked after us until the finances to support us whilst living there had stopped. The reason is; they say because our Immigration status wasn't confirmed. So, we had to leave.

Social Services re-housed us in Bed and Breakfast, only for three days before cancelling the arrangement saying that they too couldn't keep us any longer because of Immigration reasons.

We were now facing deportation back to Jamaica. At that time, I had given up studying, preferring to go on a desperate search to find somewhere to live. This took another turn as I was asked to leave the premises by the owner. As I packed my belongings and put them outside with the baby in my arms, this was when the weather started to get colder, the landlord said, "Come back inside, I can't let you go outside in the cold with the kids; if it was you alone, I would let you go, but because of the children come back in and let us talk."

CHAPTER 25

HIDDEN TRUTH ABOUT VAL REVEALED

"Who is responsible for these children?" asked the landlord:

"Val, my little girl's dad," I replied.

"Call him!" the landlord suggested.

"I'll take care of the housing situation," he exclaimed on arrival, withdrawing now to speak to me in private. "I've got something to tell you: there's someone living in the flat – a lady with a baby who got thrown out of her own flat by her boyfriend, so I took her in." *Didn't this seem suspicious?*

Val didn't want to come clean on whether the baby was his, so I threatened to phone Immigration on him. Out of fear he ended up inviting the children and I to come and stay in the same flat with the woman. As soon as the woman saw us, she ran out of the flat looking confused. That did concern me, the behaviour she displayed looked suspicious.

Given that we were crammed for space, it was hardly three weeks before Val issued me and my children an ultimatum to find alternative accommodation and within two weeks that the woman with the child he claimed was not his, could stay there. Throwing us out on the streets in preference to another woman – what was this about: my daughter, his child and I am her mother? How could he do this to his own flesh and blood?

Within about two weeks, the woman went away for some time,

I wasn't aware if she was coming back, and Val didn't share that with me. So, I called him and suggested that I was about to tidy the sitting room which she was staying in and moved the two bigger ones in there to make them comfortable. I had hardly finished talking to Val before he called her to let her know what I had said to him. He was so conniving, and dodgy.

Before I could finish tidying up properly, it was the woman who walked in furiously and grabbed me, while Val stood at the side door looking on at what was taking place and refused to intervene, not even for his daughter's sake. I never forget how my two big daughters jumped on her back to defend me. I am sorry my children had gotten caught up in the mess.

Also, a neighbour called the police. When they came, they asked who we were. I told them who I was and why I was there. They told me to stay, which was when they learnt I had a child by Val. They asked the woman who she was; not sure what she said, but all I knew was that she left. Val didn't like the fact that I was staying, so he started challenging me to leave, by tormenting me daily, doing anything he could find to do for me to give up and go. For example, removing the locks from the door, curtains from the window and sending me letters of eviction. The thing that shocked me, the property wasn't even his because he was paying a leaseholder's charge.

What was Val thinking when he brought me and the children to live in that one-room flat with this woman? Also, he claimed the child wasn't his, that was a mystery that never got solved. I think Val was lying when he claimed the child wasn't his, but I have no proof to confirm so, as the saying goes, let sleeping dogs lie.

Not everyone would agree on the decision I took to take back control of my children's happiness and to ensure their environment was safe and comfortable. I never forget Val used to buy Pampers for his daughter and want me to share them with this woman. I think he knew very well what he was doing.

I know he had the behaviour of a Muslim, as he told me he was, but for God's sake, I was the wrong woman he chose to introduce this lifestyle to. I don't discriminate against anyone's belief and their practices but not everyone wants to live like that, and they should never be forced into that lifestyle.

It was funny that I never saw Val practising the faith he claimed he was part of that group. Other than he claimed to be part of the religion; the only thing I saw around me that connected Val to the religion was the Koran and it was stuck on the bookshelf with dust on it. He never read it saying: "If you're unholy, you shouldn't touch it."

Thanks be to God for Salvation through Jesus Christ. He said, "Come just as you are." You don't have to feel holy and clean; he will clean you up. Take all your baggage with you if you feel you're weak to drop them because by the time he finishes with you, you will no longer need them.

It wasn't easy for me to let go of my baggage but gradually all of it will be gone. It is a daily process, that is what I love with Christianity; it is a lifestyle, God doesn't force you, take it or leave it; it's up to you.

Also, because Val brought my children from Jamaica, I wasn't going to let him mistreat them, not under my watch, I refuse to tolerate that kind of treatment. Also, the reader might be wondering why Val suddenly changed towards me. The truth is; I had found out that he had four baby mothers, one wife, and was living with his first son's mother, not the one he married and wanted to still be in a relationship with me. I told myself I deserved better, I wasn't afraid of the challenge, I had three girls who are looking up to me.

As the hatred in him grew stronger, I knew I had to face reality that he would try anything to overthrow me. Having the three children, especially the one which was his, made me question his motives in turning us out on to the street – another side of this man

I never knew existed.

I never realized he could be so heartless and cruel. I hadn't got the least idea that he had gone as far as to take me to court to leave the property. One morning I was at the house, tidying the baby, and a letter dropped through the door.

A Heartless Man

I opened the letter and realized the date set for a Court hearing was the same day at 10am, which gave me only an hour to get to the court in Camberwell Green Magistrates' Court, London. I managed to quickly dress and leave the baby with the two older ones and rushed to the Court.

The Judge that morning was a godsend. As he listened to my side of the story and realized that I had a child by Val, he pronounced the following words: "Stay where you are."

When Val realized the Judge favoured me, he left with avengeance. He went to the property before I got there and started removing the curtains, changing the locks on the doors, called British Gas to turn off the electricity; also removed the TV from the room whilst the kids were watching it, they claimed. Remember, it was a good thing I was a sensible woman. When I met Val and we became intimate, a small voice had said to me, *hold on to every piece of important information concerning him and write it all down, you may not know when you will need it.*

I made sure I retained his date of birth, National Insurance Number, full address to the property and energy account number. That was the reason why I was able to call the gas company to come and reconnect the electricity after they learnt I had a young baby by him living in the property. At that time my daughter was only seven months old. Where we lived then was a restless part of the city, frequently visited by gangs and drug users, and when Val took the lock off the door that is when I realized this man wasn't to be taken lightly. He didn't even care about his own daughter, much less mine. Also, at the time he was fighting me, he was the one that was sponsoring my Immigration and he went to his friend and told him to cancel the application with the Home Office.

CHAPTER 26

THE ONLY THING THAT KEEPS ME GOING

Having my children, I never knew how important they are in terms of during difficult times they would be the ones to stop me from doing crazy things, like taking my life.

Finding somewhere to live was very difficult because my Immigration status was still pending. I was visiting one borough to the other, with the hope that a door would open for me to get somewhere to live, but nothing happened.

Depression was now setting in: at one point, it seemed I had had enough. Were it not for the sake of the children, maybe I would have taken my own life! This was the answer given to the doctor when she asked me to give her one reason why life was worth living when she diagnosed that I was suffering from depression.

Val keeping a low profile didn't help at a time when I most needed him. At one point, I remember walking into a church in Camberwell, London, and the preacher said, "*Lady at the back. You will be re-housed in a 3-bedroom house, God said to tell you!*" Reader, I write in this light not to preach to you; but I want you to understand that it is only God that could keep me through this difficult situation. God knows what each and every one of us needs and we all are his children, and he will provide.

Val, The Ultimate Betrayal

I never knew that I would still experience betrayal after walking away from my first love. I thought coming to a new place would bring me peace, joy and happiness, not what Val offered.

I had learnt that Val had arranged a meeting with the Social Services for me to attend an appointment. I never knew until the letter arrived. I thought this would be a breakthrough for me to get somewhere to live with the children. What I didn't know, was that he had a trick up his sleeve. When I went to the meeting that morning, the Social Worker asked me if I knew why I was there. Obviously, I thought my children and I were going to be re-housed. To my ultimate shock and dismay, this was what was said to me:

"I am going to tell you the truth, this meeting was arranged for the children to be taken and you deported back to Jamaica." After I heard these words, I wished the earth could open and swallow me.

No way I was going to be separated from my children. God's promise, in the face of Val and his antics, to help me and no way can that ever be aborted. Not many days hence, as I envisioned between the early hours of 2:00 and 4:00am, a bright light appeared from out of the wall whilst in the darkness, followed by the semblance of a white robe.

There was no face except for the sound of a voice coming from the image saying "Why are you so afraid?" Following that voice, a second image reflected through the wall saying, as it called my name Carrol, "if you trust me I'll bless you." At that point I finally found hope that gave me the strength to fight again.

CHAPTER 27

ARRIVED IN THE CITY

This was the day for me to connect with destiny. We all need people; without people we cannot make it. I appreciate the things these people had done for me.

Whilst going through the market when I was living in previous city (the year was 2003) I stopped to purchase a few items. No sooner than I was about to get on the bus, I heard someone shouting at me.

This was one of the ladies who prayed with me, the night I made my dramatic escape. She was so happy to see me there and then decided to come home with me. As we talked, she learnt of my difficulties and decided to spend two weeks with me.

Throughout her stay, she went food shopping for me, ensured my cupboard and refrigerator were filled with food. The day she left Brixton, that was where I was living, she said, "I am going, but I'm coming back for you."

Two weeks later, she returned with a friend to collect stuff she had left behind. Strange, isn't it? When going off to work, I should have left the key under the mat but went to work with it, but this day in question, I took the keys with me purely by accident.

God had a plan that day. Both she and the person that took her showed up at my workplace. Upon introducing him to me, he exclaimed, "Why not come to Nottingham to live?"

"I don't have any family living there," I replied.

"Come, my wife and I will take care of you and the kids," he replied.

As soon as I got home, the girls were the first to know and I went and bought suitcases, before phoning my friend confirming with her that I had decided on coming to Nottingham. She conveyed to her friend that I was ready to take the risk. By now I was packed already for the move.

No sooner than arriving in Nottingham, I started connecting with people who were willing to help. Better still, I secured a job, even before informing those at my previous workplace of my change of circumstances.

Before I knew where I was, the gentleman who told me that he and his wife would look after me informed me that he had found rented accommodation for me. The house in question had been locked up for quite some time; in effect, I was the first to claim tenancy after four years.

I decided to accept and move to somewhere new. I was starting to feel a fresh sense of relief and ready to start life again. The feeling I had as I reflected was how I was going to cope with settling. Getting the children into a new school, doctor, you name it. It wasn't long after that I realised it wasn't as difficult as seemed. I didn't forget myself, I went and enrolled into college to study on the Access to Nursing Course.

My friend who introduced me to the new city was of enormous help; in fact, becoming even part of my family. She would stay with the kids while I went off to work; mind you, providing for three children and a friend seemed like hard work. However, I didn't complain. Her friend, who was a Minister of Religion, and his wife had been a tower of strength all throughout this time when I was working to make ends meet; hence, I kept telling myself 'Look on the bright side'.

Concerning my friend, things were getting to a stage where we both felt uncomfortable so much so, hardly a word exchanged between us; it seemed like the only source of life was the children. This was because she had an Immigration problem and was finding it difficult to stay anymore. She decided to leave one day I was at work which was a disappointment for me because she left suddenly.

Not having someone to sponsor me was a concern and Val was trying to weave his way back into my life. This I refused to let happen.

The real issue of my status started to affect me. For example, Val, my ex, was my Sponsor; walking away from him wasn't easy. Now there was a void in my life. Diplomatically, I needed someone to sponsor me. All I needed was someone to stand in that capacity, not to give me money because I used to save when I worked. I try to live each day with the hope that life will get better, and my strength was my faith.

Even though I was enjoying the challenge of being on my own, life was at its standstill where my Immigration matter was concerned.

It is known that many people who are immigrants talk how they have suffered because of their Immigration status. Many times, family, spouses, have abused their loved ones or wives because they knew they are depending on them to sort out their Immigration matter. I had a friend who was experiencing domestic violence because her papers were with the Home Office pending consideration.

Too often, people suffer because they are afraid to report these abuses. Most of what I went through was because I wasn't settled and everyone whom I came across knew my problem and they disadvantaged me. It is so sad because all of us are immigrants or our parents or their parents come from somewhere. I can assure you when people travel to Jamaica or most countries that rely on tourism, they are made to feel welcome, so why can't they make us feel that way when we visit their countries?

Talking about being made to feel welcome – in most of the workplaces I have been, you always find someone who tries to discriminate against me. Many times, we who are immigrants are expected to do more than those who are born here, and we are told many times we are immigrants, we should go back where we came from.

I have worked in the Care Industry for many years and see numerous times these service users being abused. I didn't care if they terminated my employment, I stood up for them. I remember one morning when I was working, and this gentleman had a fever; I dressed him and left him in bed.

One of the workers, a white lady, came to me and asked me why I didn't get him out of bed; I said to her, "He said he is not feeling well." She was demanding me to take him out and bring him out to the lounge. I stood up for him that morning letting her know he was sick, and I was not taking him out of his bed. I was reported to the nurse on duty that I disobeyed orders. It is not about disobeying orders, it's about person-centred care.

I spoke about the difficulties I had to endure because of not having someone to sponsor me. Val knew and decided to use that to try and come back into my life. After all, he couldn't help me so why should I go back into a relationship with him? Even though he did me wrong, I never forget the good he had done for me and my children he sent for from Jamaica. So, I decided to keep him connected with his daughter by taking her to London to visit him.

One day I took her to visit him, and the evening was far gone, so he offered to take us home. I didn't want to tell him, because I was concerned, he would want to re-establish the relationship. I felt just being friends for the sake of our daughter was enough for me. However, I gave him the benefit of the doubt that he could take us, but under no condition I was interested in a relationship with him again.

Even now I find it difficult to understand why I couldn't find an excuse to block him and find my own way home. Taking us home turned out to be confusing because he tried to convince me I was the one for him and how much he loved me.

Val seemed happy visiting often and trying to make amends, but I am one individual who believes in "once bitten twice shy". I believe in that phrase. Val starts to visit my home even without invitation. It made me feel uncomfortable. Also, he had the nerve to look straight into my face and tell me he wanted to marry me and be reconciled.

After the saga of living in hell whilst I was in London, also, the manipulating with Social Services whereby he set me up for my children to be taken into care whilst ensuring I was deported back home – should I trust him? I am not an unforgiving person, we all wrong one another and none of us are perfect but the extreme he went to, that was too far.

I wasn't excited about being married, especially to someone who has such a confusing past with strings of manipulations and abusing the women who had children for him. I would be a fool to want to trust him.

CHAPTER 28

CHURCH VISIT

Like a thorn in the flesh, he continued pursuing me; starting now to visit my church to convince me he had changed. I wasn't impressed because I hadn't forgotten what he had done to me and my children; some may think why does she talk so much about the goodness of God towards her, but she couldn't find it in her heart to forgive her child's father?

No, if he had done things better by coming clean and not done things the way he did, even if he had cheated, I might have decided to forgive and come back into relationship. However, when I examine the amount, he did and had to find out the number of children he had, two were born when I gave birth, I couldn't stand to live with him knowing those secrets, if he was honest, it would be more respected.

I saw it as disrespect towards women. There's nowhere in Christianity that says we should leave ourselves to be trampled upon because of the sake of forgiveness. We can forgive but use wisdom, love them from a distance. We are talking as good friends now and that is where it will remain. That is my way of forgiving him.

CHAPTER 29

SPIRITUAL DISCRIMINATION

I never knew this word existed in the Church until I experienced it. We are not to let these things deter us from the Church; it's not new, it was there from Jesus' time. The woman who was caught in adultery – she was discriminated against. Remember the woman Jesus met at the well; maybe the reason she went to the well at midday, I presume was because she knew how she would be treated by the other women who would look down on her. So, Jesus decided to meet her when she was alone or else, they would start to question him why he was associating himself with her.

My Church was a haven, until sectors within the leadership became aware of links between myself and Val. Adding to the complication was his quest to prove we were family; in other words, this was his scheme he had cooked up to manipulate his way back into my life. Once the Church got news that he was my little girl's father, in their eyes it seemed clear that marriage was the right and acceptable course of action; without knowing the circumstances, how far wrong can people be?

In my eyes, they had not even begun to scratch at the surface, leaving no less a plethora of unanswered questions. All they saw was a well-spoken man, dressed in a suit. Everyone's life is like a book unopened – how can you judge a book by its cover? How can they point a finger at me based on my apparent refusal to marry a man with a chequered history of lies and deceit?

Again, it stands to reason that *"wives, be submissive to your husbands"* holds no meaning for me if all my male relationships are chequered with a catalogue of domestic violence and carnal abuse. By marrying Val, I would be incurring further hell and destruction on my life – is that what they want?

How can the Church preach: *"Wives be submissive to your husbands"* to railroad me into blind acceptance just because it says so in the book? To maintain my own safety in the long run, I'd be better-off packing my bag and disappearing.

Within my mind I was forming a concept of spiritual discrimination. Was it just my imagination? I heard a voice saying, *"what you are going through is spiritual discrimination."* This was one afternoon I was lying on my settee and during my sleep I dreamt someone came to me and that was what was said. I woke up feeling uncomfortable as to why would a place where the outcast would go to find love is the place, they are rejecting me. However, this shouldn't be a surprise because Jesus was betrayed by Judas.

Also, as a woman supposedly 'living in sin', I was beginning to understand what it felt like to be labelled an outcast? What of the Ministerial Team? What was their view on this? Better still, how does God see me? Sure, he loves me, maybe not my sin. Also, Jesus has he said to the crowd when they were about to stone the woman caught in adultery, "He who without sin cast the first stone."

God Loves Never to Fail

I am writing to show how God's love will find you anywhere you are. One Sunday morning I was in church; feeling distressed and perplexed and decided to go outside and sit down. Then a woman, a stranger from nowhere, appeared saying to me, "God sent me to you," she went on: "You have two big daughters, one dark one and a chubby brown one."

My mind went to Lucy; I didn't bother to question her any further. "God said to tell you He loves you;" adding more to my baffled expression she asks, "Do you drive?" "Yes," I replied. "Follow me." She went outside, then opened a car boot filled with groceries for me and my children.

Oddly enough, this was the very Sunday I was in church feeling condemned more like the tortures of the dammed, no Sunday seemed easier.

Like a miracle from out of nowhere, this woman showed up believe it or not, and I never saw her again until one day whilst shopping. I saw a woman who resembled her; I went up to her, and she whispered, "Shhhh." I greeted her saying, "Are you the lady that came to Church that Sunday morning and told me God loves me?" "Don't mention it," she said. "It's God; He knows the situation; He knows how best to meet your need," then she disappeared.

The thing that caused the relationship between Val and I to come to an end was one day when a lady and a friend of mine came to the house to pray. As she prayed, I heard her shout "Pharaoh let my people go." That never left my mind this was because Val was determined not to give up. So, I feel that was a word God sent to say the relationship must come to an end.

Also, one night I went to my bed and saw whereby he was at this place, he and I, and he was holding his daughter and stretching to me to come over to him. As I stretched to go over to him, something said to me to look down. When I looked down there was a gulf between us, separating me from him. Then I knew it was God telling me it was over between us. My dreams are real and if I followed my dream, I wouldn't go wrong. Every time when I end up in a mess it is always that I wasn't listening to that small voice.

CHAPTER 30

SWEET MAN TULIP **(IS THIS A TRAP?)**

Women or Men – it is important to get to know people well. Do your research before you go into an intimate relationship with anyone. In my culture there is a saying that goes like this, "Is not all kin teeth a laugh". Meaning people may look like they are laughing but they may not be genuine.

One Sunday after church, I got talking to a young man, one of the regulars sitting mostly at the back row. Hailing from my country, a resident on the same housing estate as me. To be honest, I was glad we met. There is a saying that goes like this "No man is an island; no man can stand alone".

(Trouble) Seemingly, in his late 40s, charming enough, radiating a facial countenance all too appealing. Homeward bound often; he would offer me a lift since we were heading the same direction.

He loved his gospel music which appeared to be a passion of his; as one is finished, a next and a next and so forth; playing them throughout the journey until he dropped me off. At times he made me laugh so much that I concluded this is a real country brother. He was very accommodating, good company to be in, he kept your spirit alive, "What's your name?" I asked. This man was so cunning, never ready to volunteer any information easily.

Next, he wanted to know where I was working. Once I told him, he was willing to wait for me then drive me to and back from work. His generosity seemed so much easier to embrace. We were becoming good friends where we started to spend time talking about life in the UK and sharing our difficulties as immigrants. We had much in common because we knew what it was to struggle and experience discrimination whether at work or in the community. So that was how our journey as friends started.

I was starting to give him support in areas he needed; for example, trying to find his eldest daughter and helping with applications for jobs etc. I like to help because I believe God created us to help each other. However, I learn that even if we are giving help, we need to have boundaries. I think that was where I made errors by not setting boundaries. As my reader can see from my story, I am a person of faith. I never forget a lady came up to me one day saying, "God said to tell you to protect your heart". To be honest, I never understood what she meant but now I do. Some people will disadvantage a person's kindness.

Sweet Man Tulip became a frequent guest so that most places we went to, we would enjoy each other's company. Even though I had my disappointments with relationships, I was hoping to find someone so we could settle down long-term, and for the rest of our lives.

The trouble was, could I trust this man I was constantly asking myself. Or better yet, I should give myself more time on my own to discover who I am and work on what I wanted to achieve. However, there was something worrying me that need attention, that was my Immigration matter.

I needed a sponsor because the time was coming for the visa to expire and need renewing. Could Sweet Man Tulip help? That was a question I didn't want to ask because it can make a person become vulnerable. If a person has never had immigration problems, they won't understand how difficult it can be and how vulnerable one is to abuse.

Is Sweet Man Tulip a friend or foe? He might even turn out to be a Protector from my worst fears. Right now, Val, posed an embarrassment, more like problem number one; so if worse comes to worse, Sweet Man Tulip might be able to stand in the gap and protect me from Val's relentless advances to worm his way back into my life.

Emotionally and spiritually, I tend to be weak when it comes to standing up to men who are trying to get the better of me. I think this was because of instability. The inability to stand on my own two feet because of need; mostly Immigration. That is the biggest problem we as immigrants experience.

Whilst entertaining the view that 'Sweet Man Tulip' is a friend, what if he was a wolf in sheep's clothing? Could this be a deadly trap? I had no strategy in place to ward him off because we were enjoying each other's company. It is easier to talk to someone you have something in common with, other than talking to someone who hasn't got a clue or might let you feel embarrassed to talk about. It was long before we became intimate, and I realised I was now pregnant.

CHAPTER 31

PREGNANT AGAIN

We must be careful how far we let people into our lives. Not all friendships are meant for intimacy, else it will spoil the relationship.

It was one evening after we came home from a church service that Sweet Man Tulip took advantage of the fact that the two older children weren't at home when he accompanied me indoors with the baby bag, and she was asleep.

He never normally would come in, especially if it was late and the older children were around. I had let down my guard and that was the night the friend was traded in. When I say the friendship traded in, by becoming pregnant; it changed the friendship. It shouldn't be, but that was the time I learnt how much a trickster he was

The string of women reminded me of Val and the other relationship was another disappointment.

I was confused – why was I doing this to myself, but I was so weak and couldn't help myself. I began to wonder, *Oh God what am I going to do*? All such thoughts were now resolved in a desire to have an abortion. Was that an answer? Surely that would lead to more confusion because after doing that, then the confusion and condemnation.

Abortion is not a solution to an unwanted pregnancy. If it happens, it's best if the mother carries it and give it up for adoption.

None of us can give life so it's not the wise choice to take a life. There are some circumstances that one may claim it must resort in abortion; I am not going to support that but encourage the individual to seek advice.

Having gone to the clinic, the nurse strongly advised me against it, especially with my blood pressure being high. She said, "It's dangerous to go down that road, you may die," she warned, so I heeded her advice and walked through the door believing God would take me through again. I am not writing as if I have taken God for granted, at worst his grace, but who could I run to? Only God, I had no other to run to, everyone else would judge me, but God wouldn't.

I decided to go through with the pregnancy. As weeks turned into months, my self-confidence dropped to a low ebb; to make it worse, I avoided going to church.

With all the frustration and confusion going on in my mind, I realised that childbirth was drawing near, hence my admittance to hospital because of hypertension.

When I learnt the sex of the child, I was happy because I had three girls so he would be welcome in the family. One day I went to hospital for an examination and whilst lying on the bed in the labour ward I went into a deep sleep.

The reason for going into hospital is; because I was experiencing complication whereby the baby was about to make his entrance at 32 weeks. That was a concern to the doctors. In my dream, an Indian man came into the Labour Ward holding a baby boy saying, "Mother, this is an ordinary child."

This was more like a vision in my estimation. The actual result of the ultrasound agreed with the vision. Oh my God, I was so overjoyed on realising I took the advice of the nurse by not going through with the abortion.

Sweet Man Tulip was with me when I was admitted at the later stage of the pregnancy before birth of our son. Finally, a healthy baby boy was born weighing 6lbs 10 oz and was he a bundle of joy? Surely enough he was the spitting image of his father.

The irony in all this is that Sweet Man Tulip gave no support to his son neither materially nor financially whilst I was expecting. God provided and I never needed him for anything materially.

As the months passed, my son didn't crawl, he just walked. It was one day at nursery and the staff said, "He wanted to walk because he keeps standing up and trying to walk but sat back down." As I came through the nursery door, he saw me and held onto a chair and walked to me. That was a happy moment to witness him make his first steps.

The nursery loved him; according to them he was a joy to look after. His progress was rapid in so much as he developed, he was doing amazing.

Given that my relations with the Church was not at its best, I still wanted him blessed, so a request for an appointment was made. His godmother who arranged a special white suit from America for the occasion was disappointed when she learnt the Christening was cancelled. It was Sweet Man Tulip who cancelled the arrangement because he was angry with the pastor over a matter that was not resolved. The child should not have to be the one to suffer because of the issue he was experiencing.

CHAPTER 32

A DOUBLE LIFE

I am not here to disgrace anyone, but people must make sure that whenever they are deciding that it can affect others too. Honesty is the best policy.

Tulip, as I was saying, was present at the birth of our son. It was good he decided to present himself, but I didn't know there was another side to him – this was soon to be found out big time.

Nobody can preach like Sweet Man Tulip. Church is his middle-name; in effect taking every opportunity to preach; it's him.

According to plan, he was supposed to come to my house one morning to help with some painting. When I saw time passing by and no sign of him, it came to me that perhaps I could venture into the lonesome bachelor flat to find out what was the matter, why he was late.

When I got there and knocked on the door, it was a woman who answered. She shouted, *"There's somebody to see you!"* His eyes suddenly bulged as he glimpsed me from a distance. Coming to his senses, he greeted me in subdued tones – a kind of nervous tremor followed by a forced smile – "Are you all, right?"

A confident man was now looking like a frightened child (good and proper…). All I said to him as I walked away was, *"don't worry!"* Not much longer after this drama unfolded, I realized he was living with a woman who in effect gave birth to his child some two months after the birth of Jeffery (not his real name). Not much long after, disaster suddenly struck in his life: I heard that his motor vehicle was burnt, and his house was set on fire!

One day whilst at college, I was faced with yet another shock when I came home later that day to find a note with a crime number posted through my letterbox by the police insisting that I report to the Station immediately to answer accusations from Sweet Man Tulip that I was the one who burnt his van and set his house on fire – talk about wickedness and betrayal.

This is a pattern; trust me, it happens in every single relationship I have ever formed with a man. All these men oddly enough with affiliations with Church can you believe. Backsliders, my message is simple: Christians, be on your guard and don't be fooled. What has happened to me can happen to anyone.

On arrival at the Station, I was asked to identify my whereabouts within the time of the incidents. At the time, I was at college pursuing my education. I sought to produce written verification from my tutors to say I was in class.

After this, the officers had to go back to the drawing board to locate who they were looking for. Let me get back to my son's father and his antics. For instance, the name he registered his son in wasn't his correct name. He was operating under a different name. This was now becoming a source of worry; for instance, why is he shifting from name to name like somebody trying to run away from something?

In the spate of confusion, I was called by the Registrar of Births advising that they had found out that the name my child was registered with wasn't the father's correct name. I later understood why he was sporting someone else's name; people need to be honest.

CHAPTER 33

BETRAYAL WITHIN THE HOME

My daughters were becoming teenagers as they gravitated to their own social circles. Amongst all the confusion I was experiencing, Roger came back on the scene. This time connecting with his children, especially the older one who chose to keep him informed about my life in the UK.

Overseas telephone calls became regular, there seemed to be a relationship forming between my older daughter and her dad; the other one doesn't have anything to do with him.

This selfish man, noted for harassing me and my 15-year-old sister from all those years ago, was now holding sway over one of his daughters. I don't mind them having a relationship with him but as one can see from the disaster that happened in the past, it was not about them – it's me he's after.

Given that they were showing signs of rebellion, I took a moment or two to counsel my elder daughter: Surprisingly all my business from the home was already with sectors within the Church. It takes the Church, school and the community to raise a child in Jamaica; I am not sure how the UK feels about that. This could never happen in the Church that I was part of, back home. I was shocked which left me with questions to who could I trust?

What happens within the confines of our own home is of no concern to outsiders. I am not saying I was the most perfect mother, but I fight for my children. Even now as I speak, there is a letter amongst my belongings where my older daughter told me how much their father had been neglecting them while they were back there in Jamaica.

I am not under any compulsion to prove evidence of commitment in respect of my role as a parent. With her behaviour of disrespecting me, it wouldn't be long before she would have to leave my home because I won't tolerate her disrespecting me in my house when I am paying the bills.

CHAPTER 34

MY DAUGHTER CHOSE TO LEAVE HOME

During the time I was experiencing all kinds of stress with the likes of Sweet Man Tulip, my fifteen-year-old started to give me no end of grief. She was staying out late with girls from our church, lingering in the neighbourhood and in town.

With her behaviour becoming increasingly difficult, it became clear she was influenced by others within her circle. She would leave for church and not return home. Concerning her rebellion and bad behaviour – for example, one day she asked to go somewhere providing that the chores given were accomplished, which weren't: "You are not going out today." Her response was, "You think I don't know how to use my mouth? I can let Social Services take away the two little ones from you."

I remember on one occasion, she left for a Tuesday Evening Bible Study, and was taken to her friend's home by the Pastor of the Church of New Generation Church in Old Basford; can you imagine? Without even as much as a phone or text message to let me know where she was? Leaving me worried throughout the night, unable to sleep?

The following morning, school phoned and I couldn't give an account of my child because of some irresponsible person who claimed he was doing the right thing?

No communication with me from Church is like pouring salt into the wound. What right have them to manipulate my parental rights like this? I have never told any church member that my children were hungry and in need of help, nor have I ever sought their material or financial involvement on any aspect of my life.

One morning whilst at home, I sought to discipline her on the grounds of disobedience: as I stepped towards her, she ran into the airing cupboard, phoned her best friend who in turn rang the Pastor so a whole gang of them was monitoring my home life. In turn bringing me to the brink of pursuing Legal Action to protect the privacy of my home. Why was this happening? Phoning Church Headquarters to engage them in what was happening, but they weren't interested? Not even to call a meeting to discuss instabilities in relation to my child. So, it is not that I didn't try to resolve the matter before I decided to talk about it in my book. I went to the church and spoke to him about his behaviour after things seem to cool down; he said he hadn't done anything wrong. I realized that Church people don't respect single people; who are they to want to judge someone?

Running away from home at the age of fifteen, provided even more torment; this time she wasn't answering her phone. It took the Social Services to locate her at the house of a church lady who bore a grudge against me so much so when I went to the house to make inquiries, she told me my daughter wasn't there. I went home then returned the same night: "Where is my child?" "No sign of her, she must be at church," she replied.

By the time I drove my car to the church only to realize she was parked outside, hmm that's suspicious! Asking for the whereabouts of my daughter was a waste of time except for a wall of silence from all who were gathered inside stood looking at me in silence, no one to acknowledge the distress that I was experiencing.

They need to go back to the basis of theology. So, I went back outside challenging her: "My daughter is a minor; she is under age where is she? In fact, she is living under your roof, how come you are telling me she is not there?"

This was the woman she was staying with; she responded, "Not because you are her mother, that doesn't give you the right to her!" These were the very words that came from the woman's mouth, this was a person who preached in the same church at times, I know because I used to attend that church. (Huffing and puffing.)

The following Monday morning I was at home getting the children ready for school when there was a knock at the door: it was two female police officers. "Are you Mrs. Osbourne?" (I was married then.) "Yes," I replied. "You assaulted one Ms. Carol White; we are here to arrest you." Flushed with disbelief: "I am looking after my children; and I will come to you."

The Wednesday night my husband accompanied me to the station. On arrival, they put me in a cell and did their check and I was given the option to speak to a solicitor who met me at the station.

In little or no time, I was escorted to another room to be finger-printed and a swab was taken, even mugshots, this feels like a real criminal. For what – my own child?

Whilst in the Interview Room, these were the words of the officer: "We have had a report from the Pastor of the Church, Pastor Shawn to the effect that you dragged Ms White from her car and beat her in her head. Also, how she was beaten severely." Opting now for the opportunity to invite a criminal lawyer though proceedings, nonetheless a first draft of the interview was conducted. All I was seeing was the cunning and craftiness of a full-scale conspiracy egged-on by my daughter and the Church folks to bring me down. Can someone be so determined to fight a mother for her child? This person doesn't even have a good history of raising her own children. I think the whole thing is jealousy.

My daughter went back to the woman's house to live. This meant the woman was now communicating with the Child Benefit Agency with a view to taking ownership and responsibility, thereby posing as my child's guardian. She even now was collecting the benefit money monthly which my child told me when she finally left her home after a disagreement that she wasn't giving her money. So, what was her motive? to get the money for her own use?

Based on a dream I had, I woke up with an impression that she turned my daughter out of the house. My daughter confessed that she had been thrown out of the house with no access to any of these monies. So, my dream was accurate.

What shocked and confused me most, is the extent to which the Pastor was prepared to stand and support a woman, to go behind my back and steal parental rights to my child? Even to the extremes of concocting a story about me dragging the said woman from her car and beating her mercilessly? Are these people reading the word to love your enemies? I said that because obviously I am their enemy. It's hard when it's one's time to live up to scriptures how much their loyalty towards the word of God proves.

Meantime pursuing this matter, another Court Case believe it or not, was planned by sectors within the Church to effect child-abuse charges against me. My two daughters in full support were, supposed to be victims. In my absence, The Social Services informed me of remarks made by the Judge:

"These children seem very well cared for. Cases of abuse, do not normally reflect children looking as well-adjusted as these!" To be honest, I had applied for Subject Access request and saw where this information was true, it was my two daughters I fought to bring to the UK were planning my defeat. They didn't know I would find out.

Thanks to that Immigration Solicitor I went to make an enquiry and he told me to apply for the Subject Access Request. That when my eyes were fully opened to what had been done to me.

Also, in the document I realized that it was reported to the

Home Office by my daughters that my marriage was a sham. I was wondering why the Home Office didn't want to give me my status in my married name.

Also, they reported that I only knew my husband for two months before we married, that is a lie. To be honest I knew my husband for over a year before we got married; I really loved Mr. O and the relationship was genuine. I never had the problem of him betraying me with women like I had with my previous relationships. These girls shouldn't do that because he would do anything for them, he was a kind man. In every person, even if they have a weakness, they have good within them.

After this court hearing, the Social Services carried out their own internal investigation. Only to find out that I wasn't guilty and ordered that my daughter should return home. She remained away from the house under the instruction of the Church Pastor Shawn and the rest of the brethren, according to Social Services. Yes, the Church told her not to go back home, so as young as 15 years old she left to face the world. Do these people have a conscience?

In relation to the other Court Case in which I was supposed to have dragged a woman from her car and battered her in her head, my defence team, the Solicitor who represented me, exposed the criminal history of the said woman in Court thereby stating what her previous convictions were.

So the whole saga to bring me down by wanting to give me a criminal record for something I never did, which was orchestrated by sectors within the Church with full backing from a Pastor Shawn, turned out to be a bag of lies.

Prophecy: wickedness entered the hearts of the children. This was what was said to me when I went to this church for comfort one Sunday morning by a White Pastor. Whatever it meant it was true, because it doesn't matter that it must be someone that talked them into doing what they have done.

In the light of all the confusion and frustration coming from the children and the Church, I decided to visit a completely different environment, i.e., a local church in my community where the Pastor is a white man. After the sermon, he was calling for people to come to the altar for prayer. Upon reaching the altar, he spoke to me directly saying: "Wickedness had entered the heart of your children against you."

Could this be because the Church has had a bad influence on my children or, could it be that the demon from their father which previously had a bad influence on my sister was now re-visiting my children to turn their hearts against me?

CHAPTER 35

THE STRAW THAT BROKE THE CAMEL'S BACK

It doesn't matter what, no one should give up on their loved ones. There is a saying that goes like this: "Blood is thicker than water." Even though I am dealing with sensitive issues, I still don't give up on my relations.

A sad breakdown of communication between my eldest daughter and me, came at a time when I could have done with some help from her.

A hard nut to crack, was that pertaining to her two younger siblings who at that time were in the nursery and needed to be collected before closing time at 6:00pm each weekday. With my regular work shifts finishing at 8:30pm, how was I going to do this?

All this coincided with my daughter's studies at university. Easily enough, something could have been worked out in relation to her free evenings. "Why don't you ask your friend from up the road?" 'My friend from up the road', like pouring salt into the wound was the principal architect responsible for the break-up of my short-lived marriage, let's not go into that…

After explaining certain difficulties with my works manager, we agreed my one-hour break could be re-scheduled as near enough to 6:00pm to allow me sufficient time to collect my children from the nursery then on to a friend, so I could be back at work by 7:00pm. This whole thing, believe it or not, was hanging like a tenuous thread that might break at any moment. Pressure was building up amongst the girls working alongside me, "Why is she afforded special privileges to come and go as she pleases?"

My blood pressure was beginning to rise as nervousness and exhaustion began taking its toll – and the bottom line – I had no option but to give up the job for the sake of my own sanity. This whole saga seemed like bad timing, especially in the wake of the unfortunate break-up of my marriage – no use crying over spilt milk! Had things been different, my partner in terms of my ex, would have been the ideal person to assist in combining our responsibilities so I could still be able to hang on to my job; nevertheless, it wasn't to be.

CHAPTER 36

MARRIAGE SHORT-LIVED

No one knows what will happen to them, one can only hope for the best. Marriage is forever, I didn't marry to separate, at worse to divorce; but what if the other half is not willing to work hard at the marriage?

For the likes of a marriage that lasted only two years, I couldn't understand why the challenge was to settle myself under my married name. As mentioned before, the reason was a shock. However, I am not bitter with my children. Instead, I know now that my household can be my enemy.

How I met Mr. O

One afternoon, I just finished my shopping and was walking out of Tesco when I practically stumbled into this man eyeing me like a hawk from head to foot: "What are you staring at?" (He was entering the supermarket with a woman by his side.) "Don't you have a woman you are walking with?" "I am not his woman," she replied, "He is looking for a woman to form a relationship with." It might seem like these situations are set for me, don't know what to think.

Talk about tall, dark, and handsome. Also, very pleasant to talk to, a happy fellow. What's more, he was soft spoken, and seem friendly. Another weakness of mine with men, sad to say, I can be easily distracted when not focusing on energies to do with my own spiritual progress.

There is an old saying, "not all that glitters is gold". As a matter of fact, the devil knows what all of us need. At that moment I was going through the Immigration problem and just needed a break. Luckily this relationship never broke me enough to send me to a mental institution.

I had no idea the day would come when I was in a spot of a bother and needed his help. Whilst at home, I needed my car to go out one afternoon but couldn't because one of the tyres was flat, and surely, I called on him.

Within minutes he turned up to take away the burst tyre and bring back a new one. This turned out to be the one significant factor that brought us together with the whole thing happening so fast. To be truthful, I really was impressed that day so much, so he seemed like a godsend. To be honest he was a very kind guy. He was selfless.

How could this man be a godsend and he wasn't even a Christian? So yes, this was bringing me into conflict with Church and Bible-based teachings to do with being unequally yoked with an unbeliever. Another situation militating against our relationship was that to do with my elder daughters – they didn't take kindly to him.

A mere mention of marriage – hence my new name – seems like it drove them away! The straw that broke the camel's back, was when I expressed an invitation to move into my husband's house once we got married – provoking new waves of rebellion! They knew well what they were planning to block the marriage. They knew if the Home Office didn't grant the marriage visa, that was where the marriage would end.

Why couldn't my daughters happy for me? Why couldn't they find it in their hearts to wish me well? Great things come in small parcels so much, so I felt really honoured when they chose to turn up to the wedding! Now as I put pen to paper, it is possible they may have seen something I didn't. For all I care, they may have been trying to say, "Look Mum, this man is not right for you; there is something in the atmosphere that doesn't add up, you are a Church woman for a start."

Even on the very day of marriage as my elder daughter stood up to give a speech, she made it clear she hadn't got anything to say!

Weeks turned into months as I began to be suspicious of my two daughters. Increasingly I became weighed-down and suppressed by my husband who had no respect for God. Each time I felt the urge to pray, hence inviting him to join me "You pray", was his response, "I can pray for myself"; sharing my life with this man was tantamount to, as the phrase goes 'casting pearls before swine'.

On the economic horizon the biggest problem for him, was keeping up with mortgage payments for his house which was becoming increasingly dilapidated, i.e., in another community, given that his earning power from week to week was not enough.

I suggested we move to my three-bedroomed home in another community and rent out his house instead. He agreed; once we moved in, we took out a joint bank account whilst entering his name on the tenancy agreement of my house in another community. All this was short-lived: two sets of tenants occupied the premises which he owned, and it wasn't paying the mortgage, and the level of dilapidation was so bad that the mortgage company had no choice but to re-possess the house! One set of tenants, can you imagine, wasn't even paying any rent so yes, this was a big loss for my ex and his ambitions.

Despite all this, I was willing to give this marriage a chance given that my Immigration status was a factor yet to be resolved by the Home Office. To make it clear I did marry on a genuine basis, also because I loved him.

Unfortunately, the Home Office decided not to make their

decision for a visa relating to the marriage but in my previous name.

I was happy when I was granted the visa because I was able to live and work in the country. Whatever caused my ex to be angry, it's not my fault. Could it be his inability financially that robbed him of his wishes? Also, he mentioned I should send the visa back, which wasn't a good idea when I mentioned it to my solicitor. According to the Home Office letter "It's my favor because they granted me." My husband became grumpy and unreasonable.

December 2010 during Christmas, he invited his mother to the house. She came, and for some reason Mr Osbourne was very rude during the time she spent there to the effect he became disgruntled the evening she was returning home. My car was parked in the middle of the gateway because I went to work that day and he asked me to remove my car, so he could drive out. He was so disrespectful that she turned to him and told him his behaviour was unacceptable.

I didn't hesitate but became defensive and that was when we didn't use wisdom in speaking to each other which caused a wedge in the relationship; and that brought a separation which led to a divorce when Mr Osbourne decided he wasn't coming back home after leaving the matrimonial home for months. I was heartbroken because I was tired of broken relationships but what to do, it takes two to tangle. December 2010 saw the ending of a tragic two years of marriage when it was obvious it ended.

During September 2011 I went on holiday, ensuring my house was secure, also asking one of my neighbours to keep an eye on it whilst I was away. It was my husband's friend that took me to the airport, this guy was our best man at the wedding. According to him, he didn't want to interrupt my holiday by being the bearer of bad news. Whilst on holiday, the house was burgled by my ex who tried to deny that he did it. Items were removed such as a computer we bought and the large TV, so how could he deny it?.

I had to report it to my housing team, also the police to deal with and he was held responsible. I am not sure what came out of it because the case wasn't discussed further with me; but someone had to take responsibility for the damage done to the property.

CHAPTER 37

MY FRIEND BETRAYED ME

Another sad factor leading to the break-up of my marriage was much to do with a relationship blossoming between himself and a woman further up the same street where we lived; as a matter of fact, she was a friend to both of us. She met me when I came to live along the avenue and, from that day, she was always at my house until me and my ex separated. It looked strange to the effect I mentioned it to her one day I saw her, and she frowned. Talk about friends, keep them at bay.

One Sunday I was at church, and I came back home to find her in my house. "What are you doing in my house?" I asked sternly. I thought my ex must have gone out of his mind. She replied, "Your husband left me to finish cooking your dinner because he has to take his friend to dominoes."

Things spiralled out of control whereby she loaned my ex some money and decided to take me to court for it. I came later to understand he was part of the plan. When we went to court, the case was thrown out as the Judge asked her why she waited for the marriage to come to an end before she tried to get her money. She knew what she was doing, she was trying to undermine me. I learnt my lesson from all these trials I went through. I learnt to be more cautious with people and don't trust easily.

CHAPTER 38

SABOTAGE

I am wondering if sometimes in life we all go through a phase of disappointment so that we can become more wise, stronger, or it's just part of our journey through life. I do think, while we are on earth we will continue to overcome situations. Trials are part of life to teach us lessons.

Higher Education – Throwing the Towel in?

I would like to take my reader on some of my journey studying in the UK. I had in my head that when I finished college, my ambition was to go on to higher education. I might well consider myself blessed in the sense that on no less than three occasions, I have been invited to embark on the journey that leads to degree status opportunities, yet not even as much as a foot in the door. Some might dismiss this as pure idle talk yet it's true.

Let's take into consideration my first offer at Nottingham University to pursue a career within the Health Care field to become a Nurse. I was offered a place at the University, but the Home Office denied me the visa.

I am aware that the Home Office has its rules of vetting everyone, but I believe they sabotage people's future and make it extremely difficult for them to obtain their ambitions. If they looked at my student file, they could see that I was a genuine student. I had good attendances and grades. So, there were good reasons why they should grant me the visa to complete my studies.

Instead, it caused me great setbacks and difficulties.

One of their criteria for people wanting to come to their country is for them to be skilled migrants. What about those who are already here trying to educate themselves and they are making it difficult for them?

Why did the Home Office block me? I stuck to the visa requirement and working hours requirements, twenty hours, yet still they blocked me from achieving. They need to detect those who are genuine and help them to achieve; aren't we human and are fighting for survival?

Even if they don't want people to stay in their country forever, support them on their journey, let them give back to society and give them a timescale when they need to leave the country and go back to their homeland once it is safe. At least if people are to return home, they have a skill to survive. That is what you would call good human values, adding value to people's life, not trying to destroy them.

Britain was once Jamaica's motherland until we gained independence in 1962. So, they need to remember that Caribbean people came to Britain and built their country, so we should be treated with love and appreciation. Not all immigrants are genuine, and I am not disputing that it takes time for some applications to be considered but they know those who are pursuing their ambition especially if their application is consistent with reflecting progress?

I fled my country because of domestic violence, and I didn't know about how to seek asylum under those grounds. Also, my relatives knew what I was running from, but they did not inform me about what I could do.

Another effort to pursue my career, this time was in Social Work at another university; still the visa wasn't granted. Why did they give me a visa in the first place of study at college if they didn't want me to go further? Don't they see they are misleading people and putting people into confusion? No wonder so many people commit suicide. According to the *Guardian* "Revealed: two suicide attempts every day in UK deportation centers". The *Guardian* reveals "Suicide attempts become more frequent in British deportation detention centres, with on average about two attempts every day this summer according to freedom of information request response passed to the *Guardian"*. (Reference: theguardian.com-delivered)

Third attempt to gain entrance into university: again, I was successful at the interview and was told to send my documents the following week. At the beginning of the week, the Tuesday, I received a letter saying to try another time. Also, I wasn't hoping for much luck with the Home Office to grant the visa because my passport was with them and it seemed to be their custom to sabotage applicants. It was usual in the past for them to withhold visas.

During this process to get the documents to the University, they got lost in transit. So, I called the administration department and explained to them what was happening. They advised me if I knew someone to give it to them. I had a friend that was attending at the time and asked him to deliver the documents for me.

He promised, but the night I went to deliver them, he never came to his door. I didn't let that deter me; I drove into Derby and handed them in myself. That was the story before they made the offer I spoke about above. It wasn't long after that ordeal with my friend when I saw him at the hospital, and he told me he didn't get to finish his course. I believe if we fail, we can start again. We all have difficulties, it's our determination that will make us succeed.

CHAPTER 39

PERSONAL TUTOR TRIES TO SABOTAGE MY FUTURE

Not able to further my study, caused me to struggle and I found myself plunged into depression. Waiting for my visa until it expired at the Home Office, then I had to find someone to sponsor my application all over again.

Also, during those times I had difficulties securing a place at university, so I decided to call my college, People's College then, now Central College. The reason is; I wanted to speak to my personal tutor Wendy Shaw. The phone rang and it was her work colleague Amanda who answered the phone. She realized it was me and asked me my reason for calling. I said to talk to Wendy, she said: "If you are waiting for her to give you a good reference, she's going to mess you up."

I didn't say anything because she asked me not to say she told me. After I hung up the phone, I felt deflated as to why Wendy would do that to me. I later learnt she said because I am a Christian and I would discriminate against gay people. I haven't got any problem with people who practise certain lifestyles because I have worked with them and they can be some of the nicest people I have ever met.

The years 2006 to 2010 was one of the worst times I went through with Immigration in the UK. I was even about to be deported in the year 2008 when I had to hibernate, living in a cellar under a lovely family home. My solicitor told me to leave my home and hibernate, else they would come for me at my property to deport me.

I remember one of my friends told me, he had a solicitor in London that could help me. He was nice enough to take me by train and bus to see her. I clearly remember as I came out of the train, walked down the stairs, I felt faintish. I said to my friend, "I am falling!" I mean, where we were it was impossible for a seat to be there. He said to me, "Carrol, there is a seat sit upon it." When I got up, I turned around, the seat wasn't there. I shook my head and continued to walk to the bus stop. I think my blood pressure was high and that was affecting me. This is what having Immigration issues can do to someone.

I am now settled in the UK and must say thanks to the Home Office for what they have done to settle me, even at the last stage of my application when things got complicated. I am grateful for what they have done for me and my family. However, if they could re-examine their policy and incorporate a more humane approach to facilitate humanity and to make people feel more dignified, especially when applying and waiting for a response.

Also, if they could examine the length of time, they take to consider an application making it more realistic. I do believe an application taking over 17 years for them to consider is an awful amount of time for a person to wait, especially if they can't work. That would help to reduce the suicide rate of those faced with difficult circumstances.

I am requesting that the Home Office review the Old Policy under the Thatcher administration whereby Parents must pay that enormous amount of money to naturalise their children. The Naturalisation of a child born from an unsettled applicant, especially the fees. The enormous charge for the application £1,012 causes stagnation to a lot of children who were born from parents before they were settled. Why should a child pay for citizenship for where they were born? No child has control over where they are going to born.

***A Hard Place** – by Carrol Rowe*

I can't understand these feelings

They took me by surprise

Unplanned; I was

Will I cope?

How can I get through this?

It's a hard place

It seems so long

It seems like it will ever end

As the night draws near

I wish another day will never come

I try to comfort myself as the feelings linger

It's a hard place

But; it will end

Dig deep inside and surpass those feelings

The thoughts of doubt, fear and anxiety

And tell yourself it's a hard place

But you will get through

You were created with

That hidden strength to win

There is something great

That hid deep in your soul

Just waiting

For that moment

To rise to the surface

The moment comes, to fight or flight

A moment to cease

It's here to put you to the test,

If you will win.

CHAPTER 40

CAUCASIAN WOMAN TRIES TO FRAME ME

We cannot be too careful and prevent bad things from happening to us but when people deliberately put something on you, that's when you want to question the morals behind their motive.

On the 21st of June 2012, I parked my car to go pick up my son from school. "Lady you hit me," said a blonde-haired woman as she stood a little way off from me. "Are you hurt?" I asked. It is crazy to think this as I was a few metres away from this woman and she claimed I hit her with my car. Also, she never seemed like she just got hit by a car. She stood looking calm. Some people just know how to lie and do it well too.

She continued, "No, but I suffer from a kidney problem." Why was she telling me that? Doesn't that seem too suspicious? Two weeks later, the police dropped a note through my door; asking me to report to the station. I started to wonder if misfortunes were just happening to me randomly. Or was God preparing me for something in the future?

On turning up, I was asked for my side of the story regardless I was told by this officer it wasn't anything serious, he only wanted to hear my side of the story. My car insurance details were given to this woman after two weeks she claimed that incident took place; no, she was trying to defraud me. For a start, no officer was called to the scene of this supposed accident. What's more, no statement was taken from me. I sat and had an ordinary chat about what was said on that day between me and the woman. One week after, my insurance company wrote to me and there was an incident number created for what she claimed had happened, then a court trial began.

She began to change her story from my car hitting her, to I hit her car. The officer said to me when I went to talk to him about my concerns where the change was concerned, "She doesn't even drive, nor have a licence," he said. I felt discriminated and was ignored by this officer who was supposed to be dealing with the case and observe any fraudulent behaviour of any party. Instead, he handled the case very lightly and ignored the facts that this woman was trying to get some money out of me. I felt it was because I was a black woman I was not taken seriously and was treated as a second-class citizen. What about treating everyone equally? The officer wasn't doing that.

The case was in court for two years while the woman was determined to press for a £3,000 claim. My insurance company sent their specialist team out to my home and drew up documents and photographed my car for evidence of the alleged accident and could find no marks whatsoever; subsequently in conclusion, it reflected that the whole thing was a fabrication.

During the time the case was in court, I was interrogated to the stage whereby I felt my heart was under stress. The doctor had to prescribed tablets to help me cope during those times. I want the public to understand my story that people look for vulnerable people to attack. I don't believe it happened to me because I am black. There are several people who have experienced some horrible situations and those who put people through these traumas should pay the price.

I stood my grounds that she should not get that £3,000 she was claiming for or else I would take further action. She became confused and ran out of ideas to further defraud me. According to my solicitor one morning after the long battle, the truth was revealed: "Her witness came clean that morning stating that he didn't know her, that she asked him to stand as her witness."

Wasn't this a recipe for arrest? She tried to do the dirty, so she should be thrown in prison. What if it was the other way around? However, it happened that the case was thrown out. This situation now left me experiencing difficulties whenever I try to get a quote for car insurance.

Sometimes I wonder when will justice be served. As I said, there are so many innocent people out there today that have experienced this sort of problem and find themselves in the position of a victim. I am a fighter, and my Bible tells me, "No weapon formed against me shall prosper."

Chapter 41

After Forty Years, Mum is about to be Chucked Out of the Family House

What I'm trying to say here is, where is my mum's right after so many years of marriage and having given birth to nine children?

I was concerned as to why Dad wanted to sell the family home. Especially when Mum still lives there. After she came back from abroad, she lost the home she bought. Mum didn't use her wisdom when the person she was looking after died. She didn't even try to get another job, she packed up and went back home to Jamaica. A simple person will suffer. Also, she had children she could help but she never thought that way.

Dad needed to be honest and compassionate, knowing that Mum had borne nine children for him and there was no way she could work to buy a house during those times. Raising children is hard work. He gets the option to go out to work, she looked after us the best she could do. Mum didn't get the help and support from her mother to help her to be strong and achieve in life. I am the opposite to my mum, I am a no-nonsense woman, a fighter. I tell myself I must die fighting in anything I am doing if it is worth fighting for.

Also, I don't understand Mum saying Dad didn't hand her a divorce certificate, so how can she be sure that he has truly divorced her? I would love Dad to re-examine his behaviour and try to treat Mum as how God would have him treat her. Be compassionate towards her, God is love.

So, why can't Christians do what the word of God says, "to love your enemy as yourself". That is, if he sees her as his enemy.

Sorry, I am not writing to embarrass my family. It is obvious my family is dysfunctional, and they have problems. I'm hope this book will bring about a change, it is not only my family that has these issues. So, we all need to approach life and people with more love, and we would have a better life and more peace in this world. As I said in a previous chapter, I love my dad and even though he has these weaknesses, I will still love him, Mum too.

CHAPTER 42

MOTHERHOOD

In terms of motherhood, it could also be argued that even if she thought of fighting for the rights of all nine of her children to get a good education, she would still be wasting her time trying to talk sense into my dad's head. He was far too domineering and dictatorial. As children, none of us could approach him on issues to do with our own advancement and that was sad!

Afterwords

In conclusion, all I'm trying to say throughout these chapters is; whatever you may go through, look at the brighter side of life. If you don't give up, God will turn your scars into stars. Even though my story may seem daunting and gloomy God knows what He was doing. He can divert storms but at times He will allow storms in our lives to push us into our destiny.

May this book be an anchor and inspiration for those who are weak and for those who may need the extra strength to take them through those challenging times they may face. Also, it is important to look before you leap.

To all Christians, please don't judge me as to say why did I need to be so explicit. I had to because God wanted me to express my thoughts so others can identify with my story to bring healing. At times exposing a deed is the only way to defeat the enemy. Everyone is entitled to their opinions. I dealt with these issues by writing this book in order to bring relief to me that my side of story can be heard.

Many times, during my walk with God I have disobeyed and felt the consequences of my bad choices, but I still experience his love and I am thriving to extend this love towards humanity. In believing, God allows me to go through all these circumstances because he is equipping me to help others. God gave everyone a conscience, that is our guide. This book reflects an imperfect Christian woman, but because of the Grace of God in my life I've been spared to tell the story.

Even though I have had some negative encounters with Christians, please for all those who will read certain chapters in this book try to understand that we are all human and there are no perfect Christians and I forgive them because I talk to them whenever I see them. Don't give up on God because we all must give an account for the lives we live.

The negative experiences I had with some Christians is not the true reflection of every child of God, there are good Christian out there. These things have been happening from Jesus' days. Even though I experience these negative issues, I continue to put my faith in God because that is what made me a Survivor.

END

Sandra Niche

As the days and nights roll by
It was hard to tell how I feel
My emotions are like a troubled sea
With its waves tossed here and there
Which ceases not to calm
All I could see was hopelessness

I wrestled against the odds
Not knowing what will happen
All I could feel was despair
It was a feeling that was hard to express
A feeling of fear, hopelessness, and anxiety
As the nights get closer
My heart came to rest
Hoping that the next day will never come
And the fear would disappear
I can feel that sadness bursting through my heart
Like a river that breaks its banks
All I know; come what may
I must face another day

Hoping the fear will disappear

And hope will come at last

So, I keep holding on

Knowing I will make it

Alas! That moment came

The moment I longed for

To wipe my fears away

So, I tell myself I am a Survivor.

OTHER BOOK BY AUTHOR

Printed in Poland
by Amazon Fulfillment
Poland Sp. z o.o., Wrocław

32862852R00105